the
sociological
quest

AN INTRODUCTION TO THE STUDY OF SOCIAL LIFE

the sociological quest

AN INTRODUCTION TO THE STUDY OF SOCIAL LIFE

Evan Willis

FIFTH EDITION

ALLEN&UNWIN

Allen & Unwin
83 Alexander Street
Crows Nest NSW 2065
Australia
Phone: (61 2) 8425 0100
Fax: (61 2) 9906 2218
Email: info@allenandunwin.com
Web: www.allenandunwin.com

Cataloguing-in-Publication details are available
from the National Library of Australia
www.trove.nla.gov.au

ISBN 978 1 74237 282 2

Text design by Melissa Keogh
Index by Sara James
Set in 11/14 pt Minion Pro by Midland Typesetters, Australia
Printed in Singapore by KHL Printing Co Pte Ltd

10 9 8 7 6 5 4 3 2 1

contents

For Michael and Julia

preface

This book is an introductory essay on the discipline of sociology. It outlines to both students in the early stages of their studies, as well as those more generally interested in what sociology has to offer, some of the important components of a sociological way of understanding the social world. With the extensive use of examples, this book attempts to distil some of the key elements of sociological reasoning about the social world.

The book arises out of having taught introductory sociology at tertiary level, first tutoring and then lecturing, for nearly three decades. It introduces students to a subject with which they are unlikely to be very familiar despite having been members of the society for almost or at least as long as I have been teaching. Yet the task of introducing students to this discipline is a challenging one. This book is not only an attempt to codify what I have taught over that time, but also reflects a belief in the need to introduce the discipline pedagogically in a particular manner. The analogy often used is that getting into sociology is like getting into a swimming pool that has no shallow end. The aim with introductory courses in the subject, as with this book, is not to construct an artificial shallow end, such that the students have to learn later that it's not all as simple as that, but rather to provide something by way of a buoyancy vest. This will introduce the discipline in a way in which they won't drown, but neither will they get an unreal idea of how straightforward it all is either. The central tenets of the discipline are presented in a manner which attempts to be both straightforward and understandable without either doing too much damage to the complexity of the issues, or greatly affecting the readability of the book with the continual qualification of statements being made. The balance between making the discipline both interesting and understandable on one hand, while avoiding oversimplification on the other, is a considerable balancing task. This book represents my attempt, on the basis of long experience and much feedback in both Australian and New Zealand universities, to achieve this aim.

New editions have been prepared in response to two needs. One is the helpful comments from many of the users, especially tutors in the subjects in which this book has been used, as to how the book could be made more useful for the purposes of introducing students to the discipline of sociology. The other is the need to keep the illustrative examples current and contemporary. Over time, it has also become apparent that introductory sociology subjects are not the only area where this book has proved useful. The other is service courses on sociology in professional and multidisciplinary postgraduate degrees. Examples have been added on the basis of ongoing feedback from students and instructors using the book. Once again, though I have attempted to impart a fairly traditional view of the discipline of sociology, in terms of which, and afterwards against which, instructors can teach in subsequent years if they so choose. Finally a note to instructors—in its earlier editions, which include an international edition (Rutgers University Press, New Jersey, 1996), as well as a Norwegian edition, (with Aksel Tjora, *Pa Sociologisk Spor: En innforing I sociologisk fortaelse*, Tapir Academisk Forlag, Trondheim, Norway, 2006), this book has proved most useful as a supplement to an established textbook of introductory sociology; to be used in the first four to six weeks of an introductory subject as a means of stimulating the sociological imagination. It attempts to whet the appetites of the students for the task of studying the discipline which lies ahead. The book has also proved particularly useful for students studying in multidisciplinary settings to access an introduction to a sociological style of reasoning.

Many people have contributed both directly and indirectly to this book. Foremost among these is Johanna Wyn but there are many current and former colleagues, as well as many current and former students (now too many to name) whose contributions I have valued in improving the book.

1 introduction

quest: a search or pursuit made in order to find or obtain something.

The Macquarie Dictionary

A number of today's computer games involve a quest. In these carefully written programs the designer takes the players on a journey, often challenging and difficult, in order to achieve something at the end. In their search or pursuit, the players must gather various tools to assist them, making the task easier by helping the players overcome the obstacles that lie in their path.

Think of this short book as educational software designed to lead students on a quest to understand the social world and how it is changing. It is not an easy quest; it is likely to be a challenge that at times will be frustrating. But ultimately it is designed not only to be enjoyable but also to be a useful part of what it means to be educated, either for its own sake or as part of a program of study leading to professional qualifications. Along the path to sociological understanding, tools are available to assist in the quest. These tools are sociological ones in the form of concepts. As we shall see, when these concepts are woven into sociological theories and methods, they help us make sense of social life.

the origins of sociology

The term 'sociology', an amalgam of Latin and Greek meaning 'reasoning about the social', was coined by the Frenchman Auguste Comte in 1842. Of course, such reasoning predates this time by many centuries, but the discipline has emerged and gained coherence in the past century, first in Europe and then progressively in North America and all other parts of the world.

The 'twin' revolutions of late eighteenth-century Europe —the French and Industrial revolutions—provided the context in which sociology emerged. During the French Revolution (beginning in 1789), the masses overthrew the aristocracy and brought about the end of monarchical rule. The process began earlier in the century in the period known as the Enlightenment, during which laws based on religious principles were gradually challenged in favour of those based on more secular, rational thought. The Industrial Revolution of the eighteenth and nineteenth century transformed the British economy from being agriculturally based to factory based.

Sociology as a discipline came into being in Europe as an attempt to understand and make sense of these massive changes. All aspects of European society were affected by these profound philosophical, economic and political changes. Family, work, transportation, entertainment and medicine were all dramatically changed as a result of these overlapping historical events, which became associated with the development of what we now call *modernity*, used here in the sense of post-Enlightenment social processes.

The early sociologists struggled to analyse and come to terms with the meaning of these social changes. Indeed, the social sciences in general and sociology in particular came into being as a direct response to the social problems of modernity as Harriss (2000: 325) has argued. The early sociologists asked a number of questions including, 'Why have these changes occurred?', and, 'What has been the impact of all these changes on our society and the way people live their lives?'. The questions they asked and the answers they sought set much of the agenda for the sociological investigation that, to a greater or lesser extent, is still being worked upon today. Furthermore, their efforts contributed to the impact of those changes. What distinguished their efforts was the way they posed questions about what was happening to the societies in which they lived. We refer to these questions as their sense of *sociological problem*.

The French Revolution, starting at almost exactly the same time as the Australian island continent received its first reluctant white 'settlers', had profound effects in the overturning of an existing social order by a social movement based on the *secular* (that is, non-religious) principles of universal liberty and equality. Although geographically limited to France, its impact was felt throughout the world as a climate of political change was created, a change to which many societies responded and are continuing to respond. This fundamental change in the distribution of power was prompted by the emergence of democracy, a dynamic force that has become a symbol of political transformation, the effects of which are still being felt in many diverse societies today.

The Industrial Revolution began in Britain in the eighteenth century and spread to Europe and the United States in the nineteenth century. It is associated with the emergence of industry and the transition of social, economic and political arrangements over a substantial period of time, which altered the way the various groups in society related to each other. The revolution therefore consisted of two related aspects: technological and social. The harnessing of steam power and the development of manufacturing and factories brought massive social and economic changes, including urbanisation and the growth of cities, as the capitalist system of production developed and replaced feudalism as the basis of the social order.

The extent of the changes in the established social order was apparent to a number of writers and thinkers from a variety of backgrounds. Each in their own way attempted to make sense of the changes occurring around them at that time. These changes were not only economic, they were also profoundly political and moral in character. The meaning and implications of these changes for how societies functioned were the subject of detailed analyses of the emergence of what we now call the modern world. For most sociologists, the most important of these analyses were by Emile Durkheim, Karl Marx and Max Weber. They each gave different answers to the sociological problem of what was happening to the world as they knew it. Most of their answers were critical, and each was different and distinctive. These diverse threads of explanation came to be called sociology.

For Karl Marx (1818–83), the transformation was understood primarily as a change in the *economic structure* of societies; a change in the means by which economic production was organised from a system called feudalism to one called capitalism. Other massive changes, he believed, flowed from this change in the economic or *material conditions* under which people lived. Of course, his contribution was not only to sociology; the effect of his ideas on the modern world has been enormous.

While Marx was trying to provide the intellectual and political basis for the change in the social order, the issue for Frenchman Emile Durkheim (pronounced 'Derk-hime'), who lived from 1858 to 1917, was more of how to preserve it.

For Durkheim the basis for social order (how society hangs together and works over time) was not economic but moral, expressed in the type of solidarity that a society exhibited. Previously, social order had been based on what he called *mechanical solidarity*—people belonged on the basis of their small, uncomplicated society, where everyone performed similar activities. Integration was possible because of shared assumptions and lifestyles. This tended to promote a common morality. The massive transformation in society associated with the advent of modernity could be analysed as a move towards *organic solidarity*, where integration occurs on the basis of specialisation of work tasks, on dependence upon each other to meet human needs through a *division of labour*. Societies had to actively promote a strong sense of shared morality, he believed, in order to overcome the potentially harmful consequences of modernisation—a process he felt distinctly ambivalent about.

The German Max Weber (pronounced 'Vey-ber') lived from 1864 to 1920, and he, too, was distinctly ambivalent about the changes occurring in society. He studied other societies, such as India and China, that had not undergone such monumental changes in order to understand the distinctiveness of the modern Western world. For Weber, the key change was in the growth of *rationality*, that of basing decisions not on tradition or other considerations but on what is considered the best and most efficient means of reaching a particular goal. The growth of rationality had been occurring over several centuries in the Western world and according to Weber it was particularly manifested in the changing basis for authority. His theory of social change was that gradually *legal–rational authority*, where leadership is based on legally endorsed formal rules such as the election of a prime minister, had gradually replaced either *traditional authority* (such as a monarchy, where authority stems from family membership over several generations) or *charismatic authority* (based on the extraordinary personal characteristics of the leader).

Other social theorists also sought to understand the changes, but Marx, Durkheim and Weber are considered the most important from the perspective of modern sociology. They agreed that something major had happened to the European society they lived in, but disagreed on what exactly had taken place, why change had occurred, and what the consequences were. The basis for their analyses rested upon different assumptions or premises and ultimately upon different theoretical foundations. These will be explored in more detail later in this book because they still provide much of the core agenda at the foundation of the concerns of the discipline. The unique manner in which they took aspects of society as sociological problems has become the hallmark of a sociological perspective.

what's to come?

The path of this particular quest for sociological understanding of the social world has not been an easy one. Sociology has grown to be one of the most popular tertiary subjects for study, with its practitioners contributing at every level of society to improve our understanding of what is happening to the social world as we know it. However, sociology retains a somewhat controversial character. All members of society obviously have experience in understanding and analysing what is going on around them. What sociologists do is sometimes assumed to be mainly the analysis of commonsense dressed up in a fancy language or jargon that is difficult for others to understand. Furthermore, what sociologists have had to say about how our society works has sometimes offended those with vested interests in society and has, on occasion, been uncomfortable for those who benefit most from the current social organisation of society.

It is difficult not to be interested in what is happening to our own society and to the social world in which we live. We are all fundamentally social animals; that is to say, we behave socially in the sense that our behaviour is shaped by the expectations and responses of others. As individuals, we are immersed in what we call *social processes*, which make up social life. At the same time we are also members of various groups, hence the focus on *social interaction*, or how people relate to one another. It is social interaction between various groups that is the primary focus of sociology. These might be small-scale groups of only a few individuals such as families, medium-scale groups such as workplaces or schools, or large-scale groups such as nation states. Interaction between individuals in these groups can be understood as occurring in regular, systematic patterns over time. A number of different academic (social science) disciplines take this broad issue of the relationship between the individual and the group as their subject matter, but sociology is the one that focuses most centrally upon it.

The aim of this short book is to launch the reader on a 'sociological quest' for understanding the social world. At its most basic it is argued sociology is a 'way of seeing' the world. Adopting a sociological viewpoint is akin to putting on a pair of spectacles. It enables the wearer not only to see better but also brings certain aspects into clearer focus. An alternative pair of spectacles (a psychological one, for example) will give another way of seeing and bring other aspects into perspective. So this book considers how sociological explanations differ from those provided by other academic scholarly disciplines. The argument is that sociology has a particular concern with the relationship between the individual and society, which makes it distinct from other sorts of social explanation. In subsequent chapters, this theme is explored in some detail through the idea of the *sociological imagination*, a concept devised by the American sociologist C. Wright Mills.

Applying the sociological imagination to the understanding of any social phenomenon involves considering four distinct elements or components: the historical, anthropological, structural and critical. Much of this book is devoted to explaining and illustrating how these aspects are central to the quest of understanding the social world in sociological terms. Later in the book we consider the issues of sociological perspectives and their relationship to methods of gathering information about the world. Finally, we will look at some of the process issues of 'doing sociology'.

2 the nature of sociological explanation

In this chapter, some of the fundamental aspects of sociological explanation are considered. These are the distinction between sociological and social problems; the question of private troubles and public issues; the distinction between the macro, large-scale level of analysis and the micro, small-scale level; the issue of reflexivity as well as issues of continuity and change.

sociological and social problems

What sorts of things are sociologists interested in? Generally speaking they are interested in all aspects of the social world, 'Why is it like it is?'. These are sociological problems. They are not the same as social problems, however, and understanding the difference between the two is important when embarking on the sociological quest. A *sociological problem* is that which demands explanation. It is usually cast in the form of a question inciting intellectual curiosity. It is a problem in the sense that it needs to be understood and explained. Each of the early sociologists took as their sense of sociological problem the question of, 'What is happening to our society as we know it?'. A *social problem*, by contrast, is an aspect of the organisation of society that someone thinks needs to be addressed and solved.

Sociological and social problems sometimes coincide, but they may also consider different aspects of the phenomenon in question. Some examples will make this point clearer. Take unemployment—we can probably agree that it is a social problem, that there is not enough paid work for all those who want it. A sociological problem, however, may be to consider what it is about the way our society is organised that it does not provide enough paid work opportunities. Alternatively, we might consider why those without work have difficulty maintaining a sense of worth—is it because a person's identity (their sense of who they are and where they fit in the world) comes from the sort of job they perform?

Another example relates to the heart-rending and tragic case in 2002, where Joy Cox, a young mother, died in her Melbourne flat (*The Age*, 5 October 2002). She lay undiscovered for over a week during which time her seventeen-month-old daughter, Tabitha, also died, most likely from dehydration or starvation, only metres from her dead mother. Identification was difficult as no one knew or came to claim the mother or baby and it was only made with the help of dental records from Queensland. Everyone involved was dismayed at how few friends or acquaintances the woman had, but from a sociological point of view the broader issue is also about growing urban isolation. Sociologists use the term *social networks* to analyse how many relationships with other people individuals have. The trend seems to be towards people being less connected with society and more alone, especially those with fewer economic resources. The issue is clearly an important one in planning future cities.

A final example is youth suicide. Consider the article (see

the boxed text) in a newsletter by a sociologist, addressed to public health practitioners.

private grief to public troubles: suicide and public health

On Christmas Eve we heard that Damon, Paul's son and my step-son, had taken his own life the previous evening. Since then we have been thrust into a private world of grief in which we seek answers to the unanswerable question of why Damon felt life offered him no solution but the unimaginable one he chose. But, even as we learn to live in the new, sad, grief-filled world we appreciate Damon's solution is part of a public epidemic that is blighting Australia. Our private grief is part of a very deep-rooted public trouble.

As we plan Damon's funeral his extended family were clear that we didn't want his suicide to be hidden or pushed away into some forgotten corner. Sky, Damon's sister, felt very strongly that there is still a silence around suicide that needs to be broken. So in Damon's funeral notice we called for donations to PHAA (Public Health Association of Australia) for the purpose of suicide prevention. What we have in mind is not research into the individual psychology of suicide but rather a consideration of the public health questions it raises such as:

- What are the social forces that have brought about a doubling of male suicide rates inside a quarter of a century?
- Why do so many young people believe that suicide is their only option?
- How can we re-structure society to prevent this epidemic from worsening.

Answers to these types of questions may help us prevent the public troubles that cause so much private grief.

Fran Baum (1998)

Youth suicide is a social problem; one that affects the lives of many young people. But it is also a sociological problem and the questions that are posed are sociological ones. Furthermore, answering them effectively with research and then with action and policy based on the answers is probably crucial to trying to make inroads into this devastating social problem.

A sociological problem may not necessarily be a social problem. Sociological problems can be found at all levels of the social world—at the individual, community, societal or global levels. Reading the morning newspaper is likely to stimulate curiosity about all sorts of sociological problems. Some have serious implications, some not. A number of examples at different levels will make this clearer.

At the *individual* level, take the opportunity the next time you travel in an elevator to observe where other people stand after entering. Is there a pattern in the way that the physical space is progressively occupied? The pattern you will most likely observe (not always, but often enough to make it a recurring feature of social life) is as follows. When the first person has taken up a position at the elevator controls, the next will stand in the opposite diagonal corner. The next two who enter will fill the other corners and those that follow will stand in the spaces in between. The unconscious understanding of these patterns is widely shared by the community, such that if it is deliberately flouted, for instance, by standing right next to the only other person in the elevator, it is likely that they would feel threatened and may exit at the first possible opportunity!

This is not a social problem in the sense of something that needs addressing but it is a sociological problem in the sense of being curious. How elevators are occupied happens in a predictable manner that is curious. Why do people act in this way? The usual explanation given is in terms of maximising personal space. The elevator is occupied in such a manner as to retain as much space between strangers as possible. Similar patterns of 'colonisation' of public space happen in other settings such as cafeterias and on public transport.

In a famous essay in the social sciences, called 'The Stranger' (1959), German sociologist Georg Simmel posed as a sociological problem or question, 'What is it about the quality of being a stranger to a social setting that prompts certain patterns of behaviour?'. Consider the situation of being told a life story by someone you have never met before and whom you happen to be sitting beside on a long plane or rail journey. This example of what Simmel called a 'sociological form' is nicely captured in the 1988 movie *The Accidental Tourist* about a travel writer who advises readers on how to avoid others while travelling but is besieged by the person next to him on a plane, who proceeds to tell him his life story. It is not a social problem in the sense of it being an aspect of our society that needs fixing. But it is a sociological problem since it provokes thought and more questions about the phenomenon. It happens often enough to be obvious that more explanation is needed than just understanding the personality of the 'stranger'. What is it about long journeys that invites strangers to reveal intimate details of their lives to each other? Why do we feel compelled to listen? Are men more likely to reveal details of their lives to other men or to women (and vice versa)? It is a sociological problem at a fundamental level; this behaviour provokes curiosity and this can be a starting point for conducting research in an attempt to answer these questions. Perhaps it is the journey itself, providing an opportunity for reflection, that prompts an individual to share their life with the person sitting near them. Perhaps it is the expectation that they will never again encounter the person which releases them from the usual constraints on revealing aspects of their personal life to others.

Sociological problems at the *community* level are a little broader. An example of a sociological problem at this level would be, 'Why does Australia have the world's highest rate of Easter egg consumption (and has had for more than twenty years)?'. Each Easter, according to the Confectionery Manufacturers Association (2003), Australians consume in excess of 200 million Easter eggs alone (not counting other chocolate products such as bilbies), worth more than $200 million. This statistic is not explainable in terms of Australians being a nation of chocoholics; we rank only eleventh in the world in overall chocolate consumption, far below those well-known chocoholics, the Belgians. Why is it so? This is not a social problem (of much magnitude, anyway) but a sociological problem as at the most basic level it is curious. Perhaps in a secular society there is a paucity of rituals to mark events, and chocolate-giving has been successfully promoted as a commercial festival to mark an occasion? As far as can be found, there is no sociological research on this topic; especially of a comparative nature.

Regarding eggs, a press report in *The Age* (2 August 2003) indicated that there has been a swing in consumer demand in Australia towards brown-shelled eggs, which has resulted in poultry farmers replacing their flock that once overwhelmingly produced white-shelled eggs. In the United States, by contrast, there has been a similar swing in consumer preference—in the other direction, towards eggs with white shells. It is curious; a sociological problem for explanation, albeit one that has had considerable cost implications for our poultry farmers.

Another aspect of consumer demand in shopping that is curious is the different shopping habits of men and women. A report from AUSVEG, the industry association representing over 9000 Australian vegetable growers, showed that in Australia men buy, on average, four times as many chillies as women (AUSVEG, 2010). Men also buy more of other 'seasoning' vegetables such as onions. Women on the other hand purchase more than twice the amount of other vegetables such as broccoli, mushrooms, pumpkin and lettuce than males do. Why is it so? It is not as if men are doing a lot more of what sociologists call the domestic division of labour (see Bittman, 2004). In the AUSVEG survey, 80 per cent of vegetable shoppers were women. Perhaps, as the AUSVEG press release puts it, men do 'like it hot'! Or that the vegetables that men buy more of, seasoning vegetables like onions, are more likely to be for meat dishes. Another curious finding from the survey, which is also relevant to health concerns, is that 25 to 35 per cent of shoppers (depending on which state they live in) did not regularly purchase vegetables at all.

Many community-level sociological problems involve considering why some people behave differently from others. An example is giving up smoking. Attempts to encourage people to stop smoking (what is officially called the 'tobacco demand reduction strategy') have met with differing degrees of success between different groups in society. Across the Western world, the smoking of cigarettes has been declining. But the degree of receptiveness to the 'quit' message has been shown to vary considerably both by age and gender. The group most resistant has proven to be young women aged fifteen to nineteen. The number of them who smoke has actually been increasing, and they represent the only group in the population to increase smoking. This is both a sociological and a social problem, but the two approaches concentrate on different aspects of the issue (see Gray, 1995; Boyle et al., 2008).

The sociological problem is, 'Why is this so?'. How can this phenomenon be explained? A number of explanations are possible. Perhaps it is because of 'peer group pressure', a factor to which young women are more susceptible than other groups? Alternatively, it might be the supposed physiological benefits of nicotine in appetite suppression, given the context of the cultural emphasis on slenderness. Or a sense of invulnerability among youth, which only declines as physical infirmity gradually takes its toll. These are all possible and research into them could proceed to assess which of these (or other) explanations are likely to explain the phenomenon.

Understanding and explaining the sociological problem is essential before the other side of the question can be considered. The social problem associated with this phenomenon is, 'In the light of what we know about the link between smoking and ill health, how can such effects be minimised?'. This needs to be addressed as otherwise a greater proportion of health resources will need to be spent on smoking-related ill health than elsewhere.

The social and sociological problems in this example are related but focus on different aspects. The sociological focus is, 'Why is it so?'; the social, 'What can be done about it?', such as a form of 'quit' campaign specifically targeted at this group of the population.

An example of a sociological problem at a *societal* level could look at unemployment. In the process of *globalisation*, as barriers to trade are gradually removed and individual nation states and their industries increasingly attempt to be competitive on a global scale, the task of finding employment for all members of a society who want it is a major one for legislators. The sociological problem may be to consider what it is about the way our society is currently organised that means it does not provide enough paid work opportunities. If people are having to work longer hours to keep their jobs, could this extra work not be shared around so more people who are looking for work can do some of it?

We might consider the question posed earlier about how work is bound up with a person's sense of worth. When two people meet, one of the most important ways in which they locate each other in the social world ('Who are you?') is by asking each other what sort of work they do. The sociological question would be, 'Why is this so?'. Might it be better to promote social identity through people's leisure interests— 'I'm a chess player who just happens to earn a living as a motor mechanic!'?

Within particular societies, sociologists focus on aspects of how those societies are organised. An example is conflict between different groups within society, such as the religious or sectarian conflict in Northern Ireland. Conflict between Catholics and Protestants was a feature of nineteenth-century European politics in a number of locations in different countries. In most countries, except Northern Ireland until seemingly recently, open religious conflict between the two broadly Christian faiths has long since died out. The sociological problem, clearly needing a historical perspective, is, 'Why did conflict continue in Northern Ireland so bitterly and with such tragic consequences for so long?'. This is not quite the same as the social problem—'How can the sectarian violence be ended?'—though they are closely related.

Sociological problems at a *global* level are also grist to the sociologist's mill. One example is the debate about the place of Australia and New Zealand in the changing world order. Historically, both countries were wrestled from their original inhabitants by force and settled as white colonial societies with close links to Great Britain. However, the realignment of the world order, particularly since the Second World War, culminating in the emergence of a unified, more inward-looking Western Europe, has left our two societies dominated by a European history and culture but having to come to terms with our geographical location and probable economic future in the Asia-Pacific region, especially involving China. Does our future as a society lie more with our history or our geography? Recent economic turmoil in the Asian region as well as terrorist attacks, such as the Bali bombing in October 2002, have given cause for reflection on the push to be 'part of Asia'. Cultural and political traditions in the Asian region vary considerably from those experienced in the Northern Hemisphere. One salient example, frequently the source of tension in the relationships between Australia, New Zealand and its Asia-Pacific neighbours as we become more oriented to this part of the world, is the different traditions concerning freedom of expression in the press, on the internet and in various art forms, such as movies.

Related to this is the sociological problem of national identity. Who are we? Are we transplanted Poms, second-class Americans, round-eyed Asians or what? Are we settlers or conquerors? To what extent should an Australian or New Zealand identity supplant a former ethnic identity on naturalisation? On becoming an Australian or New Zealand citizen are we expected to paper over old religious, cultural and ethnic identities, leaving them on the docks or at the airport on arrival? The whole issue has recently become much more controversial with the emergence of ultra-conservative groups that oppose immigration and multi-culturalism. The effect has been to question the optimism with which policies of assimilation (on which the post-war immigration program rested) have been based.

Indeed, many of the important social issues of our time can be understood in terms of debates about national identities. Should we retain our historical and resulting constitutional links with the United Kingdom and its monarch or should we become a republic? Should we tie our foreign policy closely with the United States? Should the Union Jack remain part of our flags? Or should it be replaced by some national symbol, as the Canadians did with the maple leaf? Would we be better to adopt the Aboriginal flag as the national flag in Australia? Or a simple black flag embossed with a silver fern in NZ? To what extent has the Mabo land rights decision and the legal recognition of the Treaty of Waitangi led to reconciliation with the Indigenous inhabitants of Australasia? To what extent will the extinguishment of native title to land, as enshrined in the Wik High Court decision, impede the road to reconciliation between Aboriginal Australians and Torres Strait Islanders on one hand, and white Australians on the other?

Or are national identities being rendered less important anyway under the impact of globalisation, as the world increasingly becomes a 'global village'? Supranational organisations, such as the World Bank, the International Monetary Fund and the European Union, as well as multinational companies, such as Microsoft, Google and Newscorp, are increasingly becoming powerful players in the social fabric of many societies. In this context, are national boundaries of less and less political relevance?

Or perhaps the reverse is the case. As globalisation occurs, are communities looking more to local identification; a form of tribalism in which geography, language and sometimes religion are markers of identity around which secessionist movements rally? Quebec is the obvious example in North America, but such questions are affecting many other countries, including Scotland and Wales, countries in the former Soviet Union and in the Balkans. When travelling on public transport in the English-speaking part of Canada, for instance, it is not uncommon to see young Canadians with maple leaf tattoos. I have yet to see a young Australian or

New Zealander with a kangaroo or kiwi similarly tattooed. The explanation may well be, just as every Canadian backpacker seems to have a Canadian flag sewed onto their backpacks, that the maple leaf is really saying, identity-wise, 'I am not American!'. Likewise, pilgrimage trips to the Gallipoli peninsula in Turkey are now popular for many young Australians and New Zealanders. It may have been thought that observance of what was after all a military defeat would eventually die out along with the surviving soldiers, but instead it has grown to be a 'must-visit' place in the travel plans of backpackers, especially on the anniversary to attend the dawn service.

Other sociological problems at the macro level are similarly important. Has our social world experienced a fundamental change as a result of the events of 11 September 2001 in the United States? Now that the evidence for climate change in the direction of global warming appears incontrovertible, what shifts in the ways humans live their lives do we face? Likewise, how are improvements in the genetic understanding of human life associated with the large scientific research project known as the Human Genome Project (with attendant issues such as cloning) affecting our understanding of what it means to be human?

The sociological quest is concerned with the pursuit of explanations for sociological problems. It is the search for the general in the particular; that is, to consider individual experience as part of a pattern that may explain aspects of what is occurring in society as a whole. From these examples it can be seen that sociology can operate at a number of levels: from micro, to meso, to macro. Micro sociology is concerned with what happens in small social groups. Meso sociology is concerned with middle-level questions such as those within communities. Macro sociology is more concerned with the broader context of large groups, including whole societies.

Sociology can consider individual-level problems such as the quality of being a stranger; community-level issues such as quitting smoking; national-level questions such as national identity; and global-level questions such as migration or the integration of economies. At their most basic level, posing questions of a sociological nature is likely to stimulate curiosity of the most fundamental, 'Why is it so?' variety. Sociological and social problems, furthermore, are obviously related to one another; understanding the phenomenon in question (the sociological problem) is an essential precursor to doing something about it (trying to solve the social problem).

the sociological imagination

Sociology may be considered a particular means of approaching, understanding and explaining collective human behaviour. Different writers have characterised this most basic insight slightly differently. For Peter Berger (1963), the sociological quest is for a form of consciousness which fosters examination of the social world and results in a better understanding of it. For C. Wright Mills (1959), the quest is for what he called the sociological imagination. Such an imagination focuses on the place of the individual in the larger scheme of things: the relationship between the individual and society, between the biography of individual members of any particular society and the broad history of that particular society. A key distinction characteristic of the sociological imagination is that between *personal troubles* and *public issues*. This distinction, Wright Mills (1959: 14) argues, 'is an essential tool of the sociological imagination and a feature of all classic work in social science'.

Personal troubles happen to individuals; they may be a private matter in which cherished values are threatened. Public issues occur in the wider context and have to do with the way society, particularly its social institutions, is organised into a social structure. Here some public value may be threatened. Let's consider some examples to illustrate the distinction between personal troubles and public issues.

The youth suicide example earlier shows how personal troubles don't come much bigger than an individual feeling life has so little to offer them that they prefer the alternative. Yet there are also public issues of the type raised by Fran Baum (1998) such as, 'What's happening to our society that a virtual epidemic of youth suicide has developed?'. Likewise, the tragic case detailed earlier of the mother and child; these private troubles can be understood in terms of the 'place of the individual in the larger scheme of things', in this case growing social isolation in urban contexts.

Another example is road safety. In one of a number of all-too-familiar tragic accidents that occur on the nation's roads, a young man was killed on the Hume Highway between Melbourne and Sydney when his utility vehicle was hit from behind by a large semi-trailer. Clearly this was a personal trouble, but the public issues associated with the case emerged at the trial, at which the truck driver was convicted of culpable driving and jailed for three years. It was revealed that the driver had been on the road for up to fourteen hours a day for eighteen consecutive days. The judge was critical of government deregulation of driving times, which had resulted in a competitive, aggressive approach within the road transport industry. So-called self-regulation was having serious implications for those working within it (*The Age*, 20 March 1997). It appears that road freight companies, in a bid to improve profitability, were reducing the allowable trip times for long-distance drivers, thus reducing the rest breaks these drivers need and pushing them to the limits of physical endurance. So the driver in the above case, at least in some senses, was also a victim. The public issues here surround those of regulation, profitability and road safety for all road users.

Dangerous as driving on the roads is, being at work is even more of a health hazard. According to the National Occupational Health and Safety Commission in the last year data was collected in this way (1996), deaths from compensated work-related incidents in Australia totalled 2900 per annum in 1994–95 (430 from 'traumatic events', the rest due to exposure to hazardous substances and working conditions). This toll easily exceeds the combined road fatality (2029 in 1997), with many times that number sustaining injuries. A personal trouble, yet at an estimated cost to the Australian community of $27 billion each year (almost the same as the total health outlay by the Australian government), it is also a public issue.

This issue concerns the organisation of work and cannot be explained simply in terms of worker carelessness or other individualistic explanations such as 'accidents'. The sociological imagination focuses attention on the social structure of the society in which we live to ask the question, 'What is it about the way things are organised in this society that is causing such loss of life?'. Does the explanation lie in the way in which economic production is organised for profit, so that a tension or contradiction might be said to exist between safety and profit, for instance? How successful have attempts at regulation of workplaces been if workers are still being killed and injured in substantial numbers? What will be the implications of increasing deregulation of workplaces for worker health and safety? The changes to the system of awards under which Australians work that came into effect in July 1998 saw protective clothing, first-aid facilities and some other occupational health and safety protections defined outside the new minimum award conditions.

Another example is gun ownership. In one of a number of tragic incidents which have occurred in the United States, a fourteen-year-old girl was fatally wounded by her father when he came home and mistook her for an intruder (*The New York Times*, 8 November 1994). She had hidden in the closet to surprise him. Her tragic death is a personal trouble, both for her friends and family, but it also raises a public issue about the role of firearms in American society. In 2007, for instance, there were 613 unintentional firearm deaths in the USA (Centre for Disease Control, 2007)

A final example to illustrate this distinction is AIDS. Being infected with the HIV virus, which in most, if not all, cases eventually leads to the onset of one of the syndrome of life-threatening conditions known collectively as AIDS, is clearly a personal trouble. But the HIV/AIDS pandemic is also clearly more than that. With little means of treating it in sight, prevention is the only 'cure' available. The number of people in the world already infected with the HIV virus is estimated by the United Nations and World Health Organization (UNHIV/AIDS 2009) to be 33.4 million. Of these, 2.1 million are children under fifteen. In 2008, there were 2.6 million new infections. A total of two million people died of HIV/AIDS–related causes in 2008. So it is also a public issue, and one which has been used to legitimise the involvement of the state in people's sex lives. In this most private area of social life, 'safe-sex' practices, such as the use of condoms, have been advocated.

As Wright Mills (1959: 15) argues, personal troubles become public issues when 'both the correct statement of the problem and the range of possible solutions require us to consider the political and economic institutions of the society and not merely the personal situation and character of a scatter of individuals'. This distinction is crucial to the quest for the sociological understanding of the relationship between the individual and society. Central to sociology then, is the attempt to understand the place of the individual in the larger scheme of things.

Other social science disciplines are also concerned with the relationship between the individual and society. It is not the exclusive preserve of the discipline of sociology. The next chapter considers some of the differences between the disciplines, but for now the uniqueness of the discipline lies in seeking the explanation in the way society is organised as a whole and the experience of individuals is understood in that context. Another way to put this is that the concept of social structure acts as a sort of signpost to the questions to ask. As Coulson and Riddell (1970: 15) argue:

> Our idea of what sociology is, what distinguishes it from other disciplines, lies in the way sociologists approach the explanation of phenomena as problems. They seek causes for them in *the fact of people's membership of social groups* and in the ways in which these groups are related to each other. [emphasis added]

reflexivity

Seeking explanation for social phenomena in the way society is organised as a whole and in terms of the social groups to which people belong provides the framework for interpreting the experience of individuals, including ourselves. Important to the sociological quest, the pursuit of sociological imagination or consciousness, therefore, is the act of reflexivity. Being reflexive involves considering one's own place in the social world, not as an isolated and a social individual but as a consequence of one's experience as a member of social groups. The experience of being an Australian or a New Zealander, therefore, will vary greatly according to what gender, ethnic background, age, sexual preference and class background an individual happens to have. A couple of examples may make this point clearer.

In difficult economic times, when jobs are scarce, especially for school leavers, an understandable response by young people has been to attempt to improve their chances in the job market by securing higher levels of qualifications. At the very least, staying out of the job market for a few more years while tertiary qualifications are gained (what has been called 'warehousing the young') may see employment prospects improve by the time these qualifications are gained. The consequences of large numbers of individuals seeking to improve their qualifications has been twofold. There has been an increased demand for places in the tertiary education system, and there has been 'inflation' in the qualifications needed to enter many careers. Jobs that were once done by high-school graduates now require a university degree as the point of entry. The sociological term for this process is *credentialism*.

The outcome has been great disappointment, dashed hopes and reorientation to new careers on the part of the (mainly) young people concerned. Reflexivity on the part of these young people reveals the fact that their membership of the social group—school leavers at that particular time—was obviously crucial to understanding the whole set of events. A sense of perspective on how the labour market changes and what the implications are for young people seeking to enter that labour market is essential. Focusing only at the individual level on individual failings is of limited usefulness. Entering the labour market by getting a job is like a race in which the finishing line keeps being moved.

Another example is the occupational health and safety issue discussed above. Seeking cause in 'the fact of people's membership of social groups' directs attention to examining those areas of the workforce where most fatalities occur. In this case, it is the areas of the workforce where production occurs, such as on the factory floor. It is the bottom rungs of the workforce which are overwhelmingly represented amongst fatalities. Not too many fatalities or indeed occupational injuries are reported from boardrooms! A further example is the consequences of 'natural' disasters related to a changing global climate. Hurricane Katrina wreaked havoc on the US city of New Orleans in August 2005 with more than 1800 deaths. The devastating toll of human life and homelessness fell not on the wealthy who were able to leap in their SUV vehicles and escape to higher ground, but overwhelmingly on the poor black working-class communities (see Elliot and Pais, 2006).

So, the sociological quest is not only an intellectual one but one in which individual seekers are likely to reflexively develop a better understanding of their society and of their place in it. So much of the social world we tend to take for granted; what sociology can offer, as Waters and Crook (1990: 27) argue, is 'a different sort of vision on a familiar world'. The sociological quest invites us:

> . . . to look at our familiar surroundings as if for the first time. It allows us to get a fresh view of the world we have always taken for granted, to examine our own social landscape with the same curiosity and fascination that we might bring to an exotic, alien culture . . . Sociology also gives us a window on the wider world that lies beyond our immediate experience leading us into areas of society we might otherwise have ignored or misunderstood. (Robertson, 1987: 4)

continuity and change

As these examples show, contemporary sociologists are still grappling with and trying to make sense of the set of core issues developed and given coherence by earlier sociologists. Sociology has evolved a long way since those days and the study of society has developed in a number of directions, but many sociologists (myself included) believe the issues they were interested in still have relevance today. There is the problem of social order or continuity on one hand, and the problem of change on the other. How is it that despite our unique and individual experiences and backgrounds, our idiosyncrasies and individual foibles, we manage as a society to exist and survive over time? How is it that if you were to leave your country tomorrow for five years, when you return it is highly likely things would be fairly much as you left them? In other words, how is social order possible? How can societies, such as Australia and New Zealand, hang together at least reasonably well, when they are divided along a number of lines, including ethnicity as well as socioeconomic lines that sociologists commonly refer to as *class*?

Not all sociologists answer this central question in the same way, it should be noted. The French sociologist and philosopher Michel Foucault, for instance, has a different way of pursuing this question from the nineteenth-century 'fathers' of the discipline; one that led him to be interested in questions of power and knowledge, especially in the workings of social-control institutions such as prisons and hospitals. As he puts it:

> Traditional sociology puts the problem more in these terms: how can a society make individuals live together. I was interested by the opposite problem, or, if you will by the opposite answer to this problem;

through what system of exclusion, eliminating whom, creating what division, through what workings of negation and rejection, is society able to function? (Foucault, 1974: 154)

The other side of the equation is the question of how does social change occur? This can be asked at either the macro level of whole societies or the micro level of individual behaviour. Let's consider some examples. At the macro level, rapidly unfolding events in regions as diverse as the Middle East, Asia and Africa highlight this question. Can major social change occur in these geographical locations without significant bloodshed? What are the possibilities for a relatively peaceful transition from one social order to another? To what extent are those who were in positions of power under old regimes able to relinquish that power under new political circumstances?

At the micro level, an example would be the often awkward question of gender relations. Who pays for dinner on a first date? What norms (or behavioural expectations) govern this potentially ambience-shattering issue of who should foot the bill? Traditionally, the man did so without question. Indeed, in more expensive restaurants the menu handed to the woman did not even contain prices. But times, they have been 'a-changin'. The traditional normative expectations of gender relations have changed but nothing definitive has replaced them. Does an invitation to dinner carry an implied offer to meet the cost? What will be expected in return if the man does pay the bill? Is there an implied sexual contract here? What happens if the woman earns more than the man? The matter of payment has to be delicately negotiated on the spot. Perhaps for students, the egalitarianism of poverty resolves the issue in favour of an equal share. But it is difficult for a woman to ask, 'Are you the sort of male who still thinks it is appropriate for men to pay for women, so that if I offer to pay half, you will be offended?', or 'Should I take from the fact that you held the car door open for me when we went out, that you will also want to pay for dinner?'. Restaurant staff are often instructed to delicately place the bill on the table between the couple and let them sort it out. It's difficult to be 'proper' in this situation where the normative expectations of appropriate gender relations are being renegotiated.

Actually who pays for dinner may be a relatively easy matter to negotiate compared with what may have to be negotiated later in the relationship about contraception and safe-sex practices. A major reason given by young people as to why they do not use condoms as much as they should in order to protect their sexual health, is the difficulty of negotiating their use (Turtle et al., 1989). This awkwardness can be dealt with by the use of language codes, such as in those countries where giving blood is voluntary. Being told by someone that they 'donate blood regularly' in the language of seduction is code for: 'therefore I am tested regularly and am not HIV-positive, and therefore, at least on my part, condom wearing is unnecessary'. These are issues of continuity and change, which are of fundamental importance to sociologists.

some key questions

For C. Wright Mills (1959: 13), there are three major questions inevitably raised by those with a sociological imagination at the macro, or societal, level of analysis:

- What is the structure of this particular society as a whole and how do the parts relate to one another and to the whole?

- Where does it stand in human history and the development of humanity as a whole?

- What categories of people dominate in society at this particular time and how is that changing?

Think of these questions in relation to Iraq after the Middle East War in early 2003 or South Africa following the democratic elections in 1994. Or consider the group of countries that were known for most of last century as the Soviet Union. To understand sociologically the tumultuous events which have been unfolding in that geopolitical region now that these countries are no longer a union or soviet, requires asking these three basic questions. Wright Mills is quick to point out that other social science disciplines ask these sorts of questions as well, but they are most central to the discipline of sociology.

What is the structure of the former Soviet Union? With less centralised power being expressed from Moscow, the different countries that made up the former union are asserting themselves as individual geopolitical entities and seek to assert their independence from Russia. This applies not only to countries within the former Soviet Union itself, such as the Ukraine and Georgia, but also to countries within the former Soviet Empire such as Poland, Hungary and the Czech Republic. Central Europe re-emerged as a geopolitical entity from the end of the Cold War, where previously only Eastern and Western Europe existed. Where does a country, such as the former Yugoslavia, stand in human history? Did the restraint for half a century of ancient enmities between its ethnic and religious groups, which have now reasserted themselves with terrible consequences, contribute to the development of humanity as a whole? With the demise of the controlling power of the communist politicians from the former Soviet Union, who is filling this vacuum—capitalist entrepreneurs, organised crime or reformed soviet politicians?

Some sociologists focus at the closer micro level of analysis at features within societies. Again, the sociological imagination involves approaching the explanation of social phenomena as sociological problems by asking five basic questions in the quest to understand social phenomena. These questions are:

- What's happening?

- Why?

- What are the consequences?

- How do you know?

- How could it be otherwise?

A couple of examples will make this point clearer.

First, let's consider the social and sociological problem of divorce. In Western countries, roughly speaking, for every five marriages registered, between two and three will end in divorce. In Australia, of all relationships that result in marriage, over 40 per cent will end in divorce (ABS, 2009).

The crude divorce rate in Australia, at 2.8 per 1000 population in 2001, was lower than the United States (4.2 in 1998) and the United Kingdom (2.9 in 1996) but higher than New Zealand (2.7 in 1998) and Canada (2.3 in 1997) (ABS, 2001). This is a personal trouble, threatening personal values and creating a great amount of anxiety and stress for all—except perhaps the lawyers involved. But public issues are also at stake. In other words, to seek to understand why this is occurring we must look beyond the level of the individuals involved to ask the broader sociological question: 'What is it about the way our society is organised that results in the situation we have today?'. Is staying together more difficult than it once was? Are people more isolated than previously? A sociological imagination directs attention away from a focus only on the individuals to the wider context of group behaviour by using the five basic questions above.

To ask, '*What's happening?*' seeks to describe empirically (that is, with evidence drawn from the observable world) what's going on, what patterns exist. With divorce it would mean considering the empirical patterns about divorce from published sources such as those provided by agencies, including the Australian Bureau of Statistics and the Australian Institute of Family Studies. Are there peaks in the divorce rate according to the length of marriage? Is the 'seven year itch' a real phenomenon? Are couples more likely to divorce if they marry at certain ages?

'*Why do people think and act as they do?*' is the next question to consider. How can these empirical patterns be explained? Why has the rate of marital dissolution reached these levels? Is it the changing social acceptability of divorce, where in the past unhappy partners often stayed together 'for the sake of the children'? With the diminishing affordability of entering the housing market in many larger cities there are additional financial pressures, as there are on domestic roles if, for instance, the husband loses his job and has to take up the bulk of the domestic responsibilities. Is it the result of having more families in which both the husband and wife have careers? Is it greater mobility and more migration, leading couples to live away from other social contacts, such as wider families?

'*What are the consequences*' of this social phenomenon? How does a divorce affect children? Is it better for the parents to stay together 'for the sake of the children' or to separate? How are the arrangements we make in this area changing, such as the more systematic collection of maintenance payments? Is it changing the way we think about long-term marriage to one person throughout our lives? What are the consequences of changing family structure now that the proportion of one-parent families is increasing. In the ten-year period from 1986 to 2006, as a proportion of all families with dependent children one-parent families increased from fifteen to twenty-two per cent. In 87 per cent of these, the lone parent was a woman (ABS, 2007). A colleague of mine has a child in a primary-school class where the children who still live with their original biological parents are in a distinct minority.

'*How do you know?*' involves examining the evidence. This requires a scepticism and a reluctance on your part to accept explanations at face value. Does the rising divorce rate indicate an increase in the extent of marital unhappiness or, since the passing of no-fault divorce legislation in the 1970s, is divorce a more socially acceptable means of resolving marital unhappiness? Does the divorce rate mean that marriage is 'going out of fashion'? Given that most divorcees remarry and a large proportion of the population still responds to surveys as 'now married', perhaps it is not marriage itself that is declining but the idea of being married to only one person for life.

The final question is, '*How could it be otherwise?*'. What other consequences, patterns and explanations are possible to understand divorce? Given all the pressures there are on people staying together and the difficulty of expecting one person to meet all one's needs over a lifetime, maybe the question is back to front. Maybe the question to ask is not why 43 per cent of marriages fail, but why the other 57 per cent manage to stay together? As illustrated in the 2007 movie *License to Wed*, should all people intending to commit matrimony be encouraged to undertake some sort of marriage preparation class? Would the personal troubles of divorce be eased if partners were encouraged or even required to enter into a prenuptial contract, specifying how marital property would be divided as well as how the custody of children would be organised should the marriage be dissolved? Is formalising the relationship but living in a common law or de facto union, as is increasingly common, more conducive to personal happiness?

The quest for a sociologically adequate explanation for divorce would involve considering all these questions. When thinking about any social issue, these are the sorts of questions to consider in order to begin to analyse that phenomenon sociologically. Another quite different example will demonstrate this further.

Recently, while sitting in my stationary car, I was backed into by a large, four-wheel drive. The driver got out to inspect for damages, saying he was sorry but he didn't see me there (as if this somehow exonerated him). The large spare wheel attached to the back of the vehicle obscured his vision of my small car. Fortunately there was no damage and we went our separate ways. Later, I had cause to reflect on the suitability of these vehicles for suburbia when I had to wait while the driver of another four-wheel drive executed a ten-point turn to extricate herself from a narrow supermarket car park. How would you begin to develop a sociological imagination and explanation for the sociological problem of the apparent growth in popularity of these large vehicles in urban areas?

Costing nearly twice or more the average yearly income of most Australians, these vehicles have become the preferred transportation vehicle for many wealthy suburbanites. For many, however, it appears that their idea of driving off-road doesn't extend past parking on the family lawn! The vehicles have model names denoting the wide-open spaces, such as 'Range Rover', 'Patrol', 'Discovery', 'Pathfinder' and 'Landcruiser' and none of them is made in Australia. (Amongst these, the name that stands out as different from the rest is a Spanish one, 'Pajero'. In the interests of accuracy, I went to my library to look up what this name meant in a Spanish dictionary, expecting to find it translated as something similarly evocative. Evocative it is, but not in the same mould as the others; indeed, the sensitivities of the readers of this volume precludes repeating the translation!)

One way to develop a sociological explanation is to apply the five basic questions. The first is, '*What's happening?*'. Is the apparent increase in the popularity of these vehicles a real phenomenon, or is it that, given their size, one is more aware of them? The evidence is available from the body whose job it is to collect such information, the Federal Chamber of Automotive Industries. Sales of these vehicles, sometimes called by their American name, 'sports utility vehicles' (or SUVs), have been increasing. Four-wheel-drive sales have reached record levels in Australia, accounting for nearly one in five new vehicles sold, and show no signs of slowing. Four-wheel-drive wagon sales almost tripled between 1995 and 2002, while sales of passenger cars have remained relatively stable. Their sales even withstood the global financial crisis better than cars. Sales of passenger cars decreased 6.3 per cent in 2008 compared to the previous year, however, SUVs only declined 1.9 per cent (Federal Chamber of Automotive Industries, 2009). Sales have been substantially helped by their relative affordability thanks to a lower import tariff (five per cent compared with fifteen per cent on passenger cars), originally introduced to help farmers, even though most are used as passenger vehicles.

So throughout the 1990s and into the first decade of the 21st century, wealthy Australians' love affair with these behemoths showed no signs of abating, to the point where car makers have introduced a range of medium-sized and 'soft' 'Toorak tractors' (thus contributing to an increasing import bill). No less than a dozen new models came onto the market in Australia in 2003 alone, including a model made by Porsche capable of speeds in excess of 250 kph (*The Sydney Morning Herald*, 11 January 2003).

The next question to ask is, '*Why?*'. Why are some people thinking and acting in this way? I know of no systematic research on this question but when you ask owners of these vehicles in the urban jungle of our large cities why they purchased them, the reasons usually include status and the desire to 'stand out', perceived safety (especially for transporting children), the growth in salary packaging allowing vehicles up to a certain value, or the ability to tow other vehicles such as boats.

'*What are the consequences?*' This involves considering the consequences for both the owners (do they encourage a 'Watch out, I'm alright, Jack' attitude?), for other drivers including those in little cars, cyclists and pedestrians (especially if the vehicles are fitted with 'roo' bars to cope with the wildlife often found in the midst of cities!), the rest of society (including petrol station owners), and the environment. As many traffic accidents involve side impact, such as at intersections, consider for a moment the height at which this impact will occur with a passenger car—one that makes head injuries more likely. If taken off-road, are they likely to have a negative environmental impact because they can be driven over rough terrain, and therefore in areas previously inaccessible? A whole other set of consequences develop when older models become affordable for younger drivers!

'*How do you know?*' This involves a search for evidence to support the claims made. If a major reason given for purchase relates to perceived safety, what is the evidence for this? Fortunately there is evidence available from the Australian Automobile Association (2003). Under its 'New Car Assessment Program' the relative safety of different sorts of vehicles is gauged. The answer seems to be that, if not quite an urban myth, then at least the safety of these vehicles is lower, relatively speaking, than many buyers assume. The height of these vehicles, for instance, makes rollovers more likely. Safer (in the sense of more crashworthy) cars are available at much less cost. The evidence can often undermine 'conventional wisdom'.

'How could it be otherwise?' What other explanations might be possible for the increasing popularity of these vehicles? I'd like to speculate on a couple here. One is that they are the vehicular version of the high front fence. The general societal context is reorientation towards a more private and individualised existence and a running down of public provision of facilities and infrastructure. If the roads are becoming more dangerous, the response from those who can afford it is to attempt to reduce their particular chances of being killed or injured, rather than eliminating 'black spot' accident sites or ensuring a safe and reliable public transport system to reduce the number of vehicles using the road system. Maybe, like high front fences, they reflect a 'fortress' mentality—a belief that it is possible to shut out the unpleasant aspects of the reality of urban living by buying a fortress on wheels.

Another reason might be that they are a reflection of an urban Australian (male?) fantasy of escaping to the wide, open spaces of the Australian outback, reflecting our resourceful pioneering and exploring past. For those who can afford to indulge this fantasy, the thought that they could take off to the wilds of the country is no doubt a sustaining dream while waiting at the lights in the peak-hour traffic gridlock.

Considering *'How could it be otherwise?'* involves thinking of alternative explanations for the phenomenon. Obviously an adequate sociological explanation would require research to explore the validity of these possibilities; for now, they remain speculation outlined to demonstrate how the sociological imagination might operate.

conclusion

This chapter has considered some of the fundamental aspects of sociological explanation and introduced the elements of a sociological imagination as being centrally concerned with the relationship between the individual and society. The distinctive feature of a sociological imagination is a concern to elucidate the relationship between personal troubles at the level of the individual and public issues at the societal level. Sociological, as distinct from social, problems can be found at all levels, from the micro to the macro. At all levels, sociologists are concerned with explaining the twin problems of continuity and social change. The next chapter will turn to the question of what makes sociological explanation different from other sorts of explanation.

3 sociology's place in the academy

This chapter considers what makes sociological explanation distinctive from other forms of explanation. These other forms may involve the same focus of study—the relationship between the individual and society—but there is a distinctively sociological way of studying this relationship. In the same way as an object such as a motor car may be viewed very differently, depending on whether the viewer is a potential purchaser, a mechanic, a car thief or an orthopaedic surgeon, there are different approaches to understanding and explaining social life. All scholarship requires selectivity; the focus in this chapter is the distinctively selective approach that is sociology.

the science of sociology

The task of differentiating sociological explanation from other explanations or types of knowledge usually involves some claim about the scientific status of sociological knowledge; in other words, that sociology is a science—a social science. What does it mean to say that sociology is a social science? In what ways can it be considered to be scientific? Such questions have been the subject of considerable debate within the discipline and they relate to the philosophical underpinnings of sociology.

The philosophy of science, and the social sciences in particular, is well explored in other texts (for an introduction to the issues, see Chalmers, 1982). For our purposes, I will briefly outline two major positions. These are known usually as either hard and soft science approaches, or by their roughly equivalent philosophical names of *positivist* and *non-positivist* (sometimes called *naturalistic*) approaches. Most sociologists work within one of these two approaches.

The first view, the positivist approach to this question of how the sociological study of society is scientific, is to argue that science is something done by other disciplines such as chemistry and biology. To study society scientifically, sociology can and should emulate these other disciplines as far as possible. This view is succinctly expressed by the English sociologist John Goldthorpe (1974: 3):

> Sociology is the study of human social behaviour. It represents an attempt to apply to the study of human society, the same scientific method and approach that has been so dramatically successful in yielding an understanding of the physical world.

Working within this approach to the discipline, sociologists have attempted to develop the same sort of law-like statements found in the natural and physical sciences. Some of these are well established. An example would be that the internal solidarity of a group varies with the degree of the external threat. One often hears older members of the community remark, 'We were never so unified as a nation as during the two world wars'; a time when the external threat to our society was at its greatest. This is an expression of the law-like statement above.

Historically speaking, changes in internal solidarity have been reflected in parallel changes in other aspects of society, such as suicide rates. During wartime, suicide rates decline (O'Malley, 1975). With peace, rates of suicide increase. A contemporary expression of this insight, deriving from one of the 'founding fathers' of positivist sociology, Emile Durkheim, comes from Northern Ireland. Since the signing of the Peace Accord and its electoral ratification there has been a marked reduction in paramilitary violence. Since then, also, the number of young people turning the violence on themselves by committing suicide has dramatically increased. Commentators have indicated that 'the troubles' had a protective role, especially for young men, in providing a sense of solidarity. With that role diminished, and with unemployment high, a sense of purposelessness has resulted (*The Age*, 9 June 1998).

Further application of this law-like statement can be made with reference to whole societies. Take, for example, the changing place of the former outposts of the British Empire: Australia and New Zealand. In the 21st century, the similarities and isolation of these two outposts of European culture, lying close together in the southern hemisphere in a region of countries with very different cultural traditions, may lead in time to a form of internal solidarity across the Tasman Sea. Perhaps the result will be a new political/economic entity known as the 'Federal Republic of Australasia', similar to the European Union.

Or perhaps in the context of climate change leading to global warming, the generalised threat to the future of humankind may eventually lead to more internal solidarity between nations to combat such changes to the physical and human ecosystems? However, the evidence from attempts thus far, such as the Copenhagen summit of nations in 2009, to find common ground and a basis for collective action to both mitigate and adapt to rising global temperatures, does not give grounds for confidence that this will occur; at least not until the threat is much more obvious and widely felt.

The more threatened a group is (be it a small-scale group such as a family or a larger group such as a whole nation), the more likely it will tend to concentrate on those things that bind its members together rather than divide them. For example, in the post–Cold War era, when the threat of nuclear holocaust eased, there was a period when the perceived external threat to whole societies, such as Australia or the United States, lessened. As a result, some major internal divisions surfaced with renewed vigour. It is possible to say that the major threat to the security of these countries is as much internal as it is external. Emerging social divisions along ethnic and income lines (as the polarisation into rich and poor continues apace) threatens national stability. In the United States this has occurred to the point where the violence taking place, particularly in the large cities and especially amongst young men, is something akin to a civil war in which the victims might be considered urban war wounded. In other words, as the external threat receded, internal solidarity decreased (at least until 11 September 2001 when external threats have again emerged).

The trend has affected other areas of society including politics. Political cultures tend to work on the basis of the construction of what we call an *outgroup*—a 'they' or an 'other'. In the United States, for example, since the Cold War the 'other' has changed. The threat previously came from outside American society (for example, the Russians). Then the 'other' of American politics became more focused internally, on groups such as immigrants or ultra-conservative political groups as seen by the bombing of a government building in Oklahoma in 1995, resulting in a huge loss of life. Now it has changed again with the events of 11 September 2001 and the emergence of terrorist groups such as Al Qaeda; a development that has led to the establishment of a government bureaucracy for 'homeland security'. A similar trend has been apparent in Australia, first with the emergence of ultra-conservative political parties constructing the 'other' on the basis of ethnicity; Indigenous Australians and immigrants, especially those arriving illegally by boat from countries like Afghanistan and Sri Lanka. It has continued more recently, especially since the Bali bombings in October 2002 and the bombing of luxury hotels in Jakarta in 2009, with the attention on internal security issues. It can be seen by these examples that internal solidarity and external threat are closely related. And this is the 'hard science' answer to the question of the scientific nature of sociology, modelling the discipline on other sciences in the search for law-like statements.

The alternative, non-positivist approach, sometimes called the naturalistic or soft-science approach, is the one argued for here. From this position the objects of study in the biological and physical sciences are so different from those in the social sciences that different methods of inquiry or research techniques are necessary. The quest for sociological understanding is still scientific in character but what makes it scientific is not so much the particular methods used but the approach taken. This view has been discussed by Berger (1963) as the humanist approach to the philosophical questions about how we can 'know' things, in this case, about the social world. It is the manner of proceeding in a disciplined fashion that gives sociology, and indeed other social sciences, a scientific character. It is a way of proceeding that seeks explanations for social phenomena based on a rational appeal to impartial evidence. After all, this is what is meant when we describe sociology as a *scholarly discipline* in either a positivist or non-positivist mode: studying social phenomena in a particular way that is systematic, rigorous and based on the use of evidence about the world. The question of what constitutes evidence will be taken up in a later chapter.

An example should make clearer the difference between the biological and physical sciences on one hand and the social sciences on the other. In the former, propositions about the physical world are expressed as laws—mechanical and invariant. Whether it occurs in Adelaide or Auckland, in 1911 or 2011, if you sit directly under a very ripe apple hanging on a tree, sooner or later you will get a lump on the head. This will occur irrespective of whether a chap called Newton ever lived or ever developed a theory of gravity to explain why this lump will occur!

Law-like statements, however, such as the example given above, while useful, are limited in social life. Sociologists working within a positivist approach, attempting to emulate their natural and physical scientist colleagues, have found a relatively narrow range of areas where such statements are applicable. For the most part, they have to contend with the fact that people do things differently in different parts of the world; that actions and behaviours have different meanings within different cultures. A couple of examples may make this point clearer. One example concerns the meaning of 'dinner'. In North America, 'dinner' is for refuelling the body and is usually served soon after six o'clock in the evening. It is typically one course, with all the food on one plate, served without alcohol, and completed inside half an hour. There are, of course, exceptions, but this is how most people there take their main meal of the day. In Europe, by contrast, the meaning of dinner is cast not only around refuelling but also as a means of socialising. Eaten later (as late as nine or ten o'clock in countries such as Spain), it involves several courses over more than an hour, with alcohol consumed by everyone, even by children, who drink it in small quantities or diluted. In North America giving your child a glass of wine with dinner would be defined by many as akin to child abuse! Australasia, at the crossroads of these two cultures, has adopted some dining customs from each. In some Australian households dinner may be eaten at different times, depending on other commitments. For some it may be eaten in front of the television while for others an emphasis is put on the family sitting down together around a dining table and eating while catching up with the day's events. In other words, in attempting to understand behaviour we cannot take for granted that the meaning of actions is always the same.

Another example is the social construction of the meaning of the categories of plants and animals that are known as 'weeds' and 'vermin'. Under what circumstances does a plant or animal come to be defined as such, and how does that definition change over time? The pejorative meaning (inviting justified destruction) varies over time, between societies and within different geographical areas. Pests and weeds from this point of view can be defined as animals and plants that just happen to be in the wrong place. Think of the 'positioning' of plants and animals, be they dingoes, cane toads, gorse or *pinus radiata* trees. Or the difference in the positioning of possums in Australia and New Zealand—cute furry little native animals in the former; bloody pests wreaking untold ecological damage and a resource to be made into garments in the other. One country's pest may be another's endangered species! Likewise, it is challenging to one's sense of being an Australian when you visit places, such as California, where you are harangued by the locals about those iconic trees of the Australian bush, the *Eucalyptus* species, being weeds.

Even the social meaning attributed to an object or item can vary according to the circumstance. Consider the plant *Echium plantagineum*. This pretty purple-flowered plant is a native of Mediterranean countries and it was introduced as a nursery plant into Australia in the mid-nineteenth century. Originally it was known to exotic plant sellers as 'Riverina bluebell'. However, it has become another of those ecological disasters, just like cane toads and rabbits, with which the history of rural Australia is littered. One of its inherent features is that it produces a large number of seeds and when introduced it soon escaped domestic gardens to spread rapidly throughout southern Australia. For many it was defined as a 'weed' against which control measures needed to be taken. But the social construction of the meaning of this little plant varies there as well. Because it is mildly toxic to cattle and horses, in primarily cattle grazing areas such as northern Victoria it has become known as 'Paterson's curse'. In the sheep country further west towards South Australia it is less toxic and the sheep eat it when there is no other feed. As a result, its meaning there was constructed more positively as 'Salvation Jane'. Others also regard the plant positively. It is favoured by apiarists as producing some of the best honey (not surprisingly it is usually sold under the 'salvation' rather than 'curse' label). For photographers it also is a sought-after subject as it contrasts well with golden fields of canola and so on. So what this plant 'means' depends on who is doing the defining; that is, we say it is *socially constructed*.

Another example is the different responses often made to being asked questions in Indigenous and white cultures. In white European culture, not answering a question put to you is considered rude. In Indigenous Australian culture, however, where greater emphasis is put upon keeping the peace, it may be acceptable not to answer questions if the answer will make trouble (Eades, 1985). Likewise, the term 'brother' has a much wider applicability than in white culture and may be used to refer, amongst others, to cousins (Koch, 1985). So the meaning of actions and terms will vary cross-culturally.

To return to the gravity example, in the physical sciences it is absurd to ask what the apple *means* by falling. In the social sciences, by contrast, to ask what is the meaning of different actions, such as smiling, is a very important question. Also, apples continue to fall independent of our knowledge of the theory of gravity, whereas people may and often do change their behaviour as a result of sociological knowledge.

Think of the roles of men and women in Western society. Throughout this century there has been a gradual recognition by many women, and some men, that beliefs about what is 'natural' for men and women to do beyond the basic facts of human reproduction are not in some way biologically determined as was once believed, but are socially constructed. That is, they derive culturally from our understanding of how the world works. Think, for example, how far we have come since the nineteenth century when the prevailing belief, strongly reinforced by the doctors of the time, was an insistence that a woman's ovaries determined her physical, intellectual and emotional behaviour. This belief was used by men to oppose women studying at university and exclude women from entering professions such as medicine (Smith-Rosenberg and Rosenberg, 1973). When these theories were proved to be nonsense, ovaries went on working as they had always done, but women began to behave differently, demanding the right to vote, to receive a university education and to work in a wider range of occupations, including the professions. A social movement towards changing relations between the sexes was thus set in motion and has been one of the really important areas of social change in the past century. In other words, there are crucial differences in the subject matters of the physical and biological sciences on one hand and the social sciences on the other.

Because of these differences, different methods of going about studying each are necessary. To put it another way, there cannot be a unity of scientific method between the physical and social sciences. The subject matter is sufficiently different to require different methods of investigation. What then makes the sociological quest a scientific one in either its 'hard science' or 'soft science' mode? As Peter Berger (1963: 27) argues, it is the particular way the understanding of society is approached:

> The sociologist then is someone concerned with understanding society in a disciplined way. The nature of the discipline is scientific . . . one of the main characteristics of this scientific frame of reference is that operations are bound by certain rules of evidence.

The concern is with *empirical* evidence; evidence based on observable experience of the social world, in order to back up claims made about the social world.

distinguishing sociological explanation

At this stage in the quest to understand the nature of sociological explanation, we can begin by distinguishing it from types of knowledge that are *metaphysical*, that is, not empirically based. Sociological explanation can be distinguished from all non-empirically based types of knowledge, such as fortune-telling, and also from religious knowledge. For example, the existence of a supernatural being such as God in the Christian religion cannot be empirically established. One either takes it on the basis of faith or not. Nothing in sociology is taken on faith (which is not to say that many sociologists in their personal lives are not themselves religious). This follows from the emergence of the discipline as a distinctively modern, secular knowledge of human society and human social relationships during the period following the French and Industrial revolutions we spoke about in the introduction. This emergence was only possible in a world that had rejected the absolute basis of any religious authority.

How can sociology be distinguished from other pursuits such as journalism? Both activities analyse what is occurring in society, and some journalists display effective sociological imagination. But in general they analyse society in different ways. First, sociology claims a kind of knowledge about society that is *objective*, in the sense of being impartial and independent. In contrast, journalists, broadly speaking, write about society in a way determined by the need to sell newspapers or maintain ratings. At times, therefore, they may be less than objective in terms of the stories chosen for investigation and reporting, or the need to avoid casting the owners of the media outlet in an unfavourable light.

Second, by writing about the world around us and about what we call commonsense knowledge and understanding of that world, the approach to writing is somewhat different. Journalists, for the most part, use commonsense concepts to analyse this social world, which itself is riddled with prejudices, especially cultural ones. Sociologists, on the other hand, attempt to escape (with varying degrees of success) these limitations with demands for logical argument, empirical evidence and, most importantly, the use of a precise language to analyse what is occurring.

The frequent use by sociologists of a somewhat different language from the one journalists use to analyse social life raises the so-called jargon issue. Already in this book a considerable number of terms have been highlighted that may not be familiar to a newcomer to the discipline. While all occupational groups use a specialised language, sociology is sometimes criticised for using an obscure language to talk about things that are assumed to be commonsense. While the use of a specialised language can be, and sometimes is, overdone or carried to unnecessary lengths, its use is important as it is aiming at a more exact, precise and thus more satisfactory understanding of the phenomenon in question. Much sociological insight is what Randall Collins (1982: vi) calls 'non-obvious'. He argues:

> Sociology does know some important principles of how the world operates. These are not just matters of conceptualisation and definition. They tell us why things happen in certain ways rather than others, and they go beyond the surface of ordinary belief. The principles had to be discovered by professional scholars, including some of the major thinkers of the past; they are by no means obvious.

Sociological concepts and a more specialised language generally are some of the tools by which these sociological insights are achieved and differentiate sociology from journalism. Their use facilitates the process of *generalisation*, crucial to the search for patterns and ultimately to the sociological quest. Asking the question, 'To what extent can we generalise?', involves addressing the question of how much of what occurs to individuals can be said to apply also to groups. Sociologists are cautious about overgeneralising and the use of a more specialised and precise language is a means by which they pursue this caution. Consider some examples beginning with the terminology frequently used

57/13

to describe groups in our society. These terms may include 'skater', 'rapper', 'nerd', 'bogan', 'homeboy', 'emo', 'generation X' and 'Y' to name just a few. These terms are not usually carefully defined and are often used to label whole groups of people whose members have little in common, or are used in a way that says as much about those applying the label as those to whom the label is supposed to apply. Crucial to the quest for sociological understanding of the individual and society is this concern with careful enunciation of exactly what one is talking about. A specialised language is the result.

An example of the need for a specialised language is the ambiguity with which the term 'ethnic' is often used in everyday language to apply to all people whose family history in the society to which they have migrated stretches less than two generations and whose original language was not English. The use of this term, however, is based on a misunderstanding of ethnicity. Everyone has an ethnic background; long-term residents as much as more recent arrivals. Aiming at preciseness, sociologists commonly refer to the above group as people of non-English speaking background (often using the acronym NESB). We also need to be aware of how the term is caught up in what are basically political and social processes of inclusion or exclusion from social groups.

The need for precision as a basis for analysis is also evident when new aspects of the social organisation of a society become apparent, for which we may lack a suitable term or concept. A couple of examples will illustrate this point. Of all those couples who married in 2008, nearly 78 per cent had cohabited prior to marriage. This compares to 31 per cent of couples who got married in 1981 (ABS, 2009). How would you introduce a person with whom you are emotionally involved in a cohabiting, de-facto relationship but with whom you have not actually committed matrimony? People in this category are a sizeable group of the population. 'This is my boyfriend/girlfriend' is hardly appropriate when you are in your twenties (or forties). 'My lover/mistress' may be a bit old-fashioned. 'My roommate' hardly conveys the exact nature of your relationship. 'My spouse' has overtones of wedding bells. 'My bedmate' may not be exactly what you want. 'My beau' or 'my significant other' are occasionally used. Perhaps 'my partner' is beginning to fill the gap in the language. But until a term comes to have a commonsense meaning which everyone understands, the awkwardness of the need to state the extent of your pairing with someone continues.

A second example of a need for an appropriate term that has been slow to emerge is with what are called 'kin-like friends'. In a society characterised by high levels of mobility (that is, people moving around a lot), with both internal and inter-country migration, traditional kinship ties are loosened. In this case, individuals and families often develop friendships that replace or supplement traditional kinship arrangements. In times of crisis, it may be these friends you call upon rather than your kinsfolk. Yet we lack a term to describe the exact nature of the relationship of being more than friends but not quite family.

Not only do we lack appropriate terms in some areas, but those that are used in everyday life may be subject to ambiguous usage. An example is the term 'profession'. It is widely used in its commonsense meaning to refer to supposedly special sorts of occupations more worthy and of higher status than mere jobs. The usage is very confused, however. Indeed, it is frequently claimed by occupations in an attempt to secure certain advantages in the labour market: 'We are a profession and therefore . . .' is a common expression of this view. Using the term in relation to occupations traditionally thought of as professions, such as medicine and law is not controversial, but beyond that the agreement ends. Not only do we have the 'world's oldest profession' (sex workers) laying claim to the title but in recent years a range of occupations as diverse as jockeys and salespeople have laid claim to the term. Aiming at precision, sociologists have tried to refine the usage of the term, though there is considerable disagreement about what the defining characteristics should be. The most common view perhaps, espoused by the American sociologist Eliot Freidson (1986: 123), is that the term should refer only to those whose livelihood is earned on the basis of credentials (qualifications, etc.) that they have gained through higher education. The original meaning is used but it is now carefully defined.

Then there are terms which become out of date but are still used due to a lack of a suitable alternative. Describing countries as belonging to 'the third world' is one such term, which is no longer appropriate these days. Formerly the term referred to those poorer countries, usually less 'developed', in Asia, Africa and Central and South America, whose economies were still heavily dependent on agriculture. But it no longer makes sense to refer to the first world (the developed capitalist economies) or the second world (the communist countries of the Cold War era). Nor is 'developed' or 'underdeveloped' a particularly useful distinction—many countries of the former Soviet Empire under any criteria would be considered in the category of what used to be called 'third world' on the basis of development. Likewise, some countries that formerly were in the underdeveloped group, such as Singapore, now have per-capita incomes that exceed those in some formerly 'first world' countries such as New Zealand. Clearly some term that precisely describes the relationship between different countries in a manner which reflects post–Cold War reality is needed.

So, in common with other academic disciplines, sociology has developed a specialised language to help in accurately analysing social life. As a result, journalistic and sociological accounts of the same phenomenon can read quite differently, in part because of the different purposes for which they are written.

Sociological explanation must also be differentiated from the sorts of explanations provided by other academic disciplines. The study of society is not the exclusive preserve of sociology but is a feature of all social sciences. How does sociological explanation differ from those of related social sciences? The areas of overlap are considerable: the study of social life cannot be easily compartmentalised so the boundaries between disciplines are loosely drawn. The difference is more often a matter of emphasis and orientation resulting from their different historical origins than of substance.

Psychology is perhaps the academic discipline with which sociology is most often confused, though many psychologists prefer to designate themselves as behavioural, rather than social, scientists. Certainly when asked what sociology is, people often contrast it with psychology to differentiate its approach. The discipline of psychology in some ways bridges the natural and social sciences; its specialties range from neuropsychology at the end of the spectrum closest to biology, to behavioural and social psychology at the end closest to sociology. Insofar as it is possible to generalise about such a diverse discipline, psychology is more concerned with the study of individual human social behaviour while sociology delves more into group or collective social behaviour, as well as how the individual relates to the whole. For example, approaching the suicide phenomenon discussed earlier, sociologically you would focus on the fact of people's membership of social groups. None of the questions raised in

Fran Baum's article (see Chapter 2) related to the individual frame of mind of those who commit suicide. This is not to say these questions are not relevant or important; just that the sociological focus is different.

As with the boundaries between all social science disciplines, there is a considerable area of overlap between sociology and psychology. Small-group sociology shades into social psychology, with its focus on how the social context of behaviour shapes personality and individual behaviour. It is common in universities for social psychology to be taught within sociology departments. Sociology and psychology also share some of their historic influences. Sigmund Freud, better known as a founder modern psychology, is also important to the discipline of sociology.

One area of difference between the two disciplines is in the traditional focus taken in the major intellectual debate about the relative importance of hereditary factors and the environment in determining behavioural outcomes. Is the way a child turns out when they grow up more the result of nature or nurture? Is the outcome because of what they inherit or what sociologists call the process of *socialisation*? It is a complex debate and difficult to summarise accurately in a brief treatise. While both disciplines acknowledge the importance of both sides of the debate, it is generally the case that psychologists (at least those who study behaviour) tend to stress the interaction between the biological aspects (especially response and instinct) and the social (their term being 'social conditioning') aspects. By contrast, sociologists tend to stress the social environment. Sociologists tend to emphasise how individual uniqueness is shaped by social life, particularly relationships with others, and especially those relationships beyond direct face-to-face ones. Sociologists tend to argue that we do not get very far in our understanding of human behaviour by considering only the properties of individuals; rather, it is necessary to consider the interaction of the individual with the society of which that individual is a part, especially the relationships that directly connect people. The implications of failing to do this will be addressed later in this chapter.

How does sociology differ from the other social sciences? *Political science* takes as its main emphasis the political aspects of the organisation of society, focusing especially on the manner in which power is manifested in the organisation of society through political behaviour and different forms of government. *Geography* draws on sociology and other social sciences in order to inform its orientation towards the study of relationships between the physical and human world. *Economics* concentrates on the economic relationships that exist between individuals and between groups of individuals of all sizes, from small numbers of people to whole nations. The study of how goods and services are produced, distributed and consumed involves examining the economic aspects of social life.

The closest relatives to sociology are history and anthropology. *History* is particularly close to sociology as both these social sciences, in general, have become more concerned with understanding the historical antecedents of social organisation of various kinds. This issue of identifying the historical antecedents is one of the ways in which sociologist C. Wright Mills has identified the centrality of the study of the relationship between the individual and society as the hallmark of the sociological imagination. For him, this involves the study of the relationship between biography and history: the place of individual biographies in the larger scheme of things, which necessarily has a historical component.

With *anthropology*, sociology has perhaps the closest relationship, often being institutionally located within the same university department. From its origins in the study of other cultures in the era of colonialism (it used to be said that anthropologists studied only those societies that didn't have dry-cleaning), anthropology has now effectively become comparative sociology. Taking culture as one of its central organising foci and, nowadays, studying both tribal and non-Western societies as well as our own society, many social anthropologists are indistinguishable from their sociologist colleagues.

In some universities sociology is located with *social work*, but the two are not the same even though they are sometimes assumed to be so. As Peter Berger (1963: 15) has argued, social work is a practice in society whereas sociology is more of an attempt to understand society. Sociology is one of the disciplines (along with psychology) in which aspiring social workers should receive training. But there is nothing inherent in the aim of understanding how the social world works that inevitably leads to a particular practice.

So sociological explanation can be distinguished from other forms of explanation, both of a social scientific nature and of an unscientific nature. From the latter, differentiation is possible because sociological explanation depends on the use of empirical evidence. For other social sciences, while acknowledging the considerable overlap between the different disciplines, and, in some senses, the artificial nature of the distinctions anyway, the difference between sociological and other types of explanation is largely one of emphasis.

social structure

Like all the social sciences, sociology is concerned with the relationship between the individual and society. The uniqueness of the sociological, though, compared with other sorts of explanation, lies in the manner in which the understanding of social phenomena is sought in the organisation of society as a whole—usually referred to as the *social structure* of society. This concept is defined in terms of the patterns of relationships, which are both persistent and systematic, between the different parts of a society.

The social structure is comprised of different *social institutions* that are regular, organised patterns of social behaviour, such as universities or hospitals. Social structure and social institutions, it is important to note, are not fixed, unchanging, monolithic entities resulting in a neat organisation of society. Rather, they allow for fluidity, diversity and conflict, as well as change in the sense of taking on new forms. Furthermore, focusing on the social structural level of analysis is not to deny the relevance of an understanding of the activities of individuals, but to argue for the primacy (what comes first) of the group level of analysis. Hence the concept of the social structure is a crucial one for sociology, acting as a kind of signpost to the kinds of questions to be asked, in particular, 'What is it about the way our society is organised that results in this or that phenomenon occurring?'.

contradiction

The social structural feature of sociological explanation raises the issue of the extent to which the relationship between the individual and society may be a conflicting one. The notion of *contradiction* (sometimes called a *tension* or *paradox*) is an important one in the social sciences. The foundations of this issue are philosophical, based on this important question: 'What extent of group-level organisation is most consistent with individual freedom and happiness?', or put another way, 'What sort of controls on individuals are necessary in order to maximise the so-called common good?'. This vexed and complex question has to do with the relationship of the individual to the larger society.

Consider the high population densities in today's urban environments. As the population structure changes towards more single-person households and the price of land near to the centre of the cities escalates, government policies to encourage higher density housing (by changing the building regulations, for instance, to allow people to build right on their boundary fence) are further adding to this density. Conflicts within body corporate committees that manage apartment living or between neighbours, generally over privacy issues, are now an everyday occurrence. To what extent should people be allowed to play loud music late at night, burn garbage in their backyards, keep several large guard dogs who bark at the constant sounds of other people, build extensions onto their houses which block out the sun for neighbours, or put up so many Christmas lights that the neighbours complain?

The need to surrender some individuality in the interests of social harmony is well recognised. Should one light a fire on a cold evening when a smog alert for the city has been broadcast? Already in some cities the aesthetic pleasure of an open fire is banned on the grounds of pollution. As inner-city populations increase it is inevitable that someone will end up with their windows only a few metres from someone else's chimney, so the former may get a house full of smoke every time their neighbours light a fire. Similarly, in many places the police will act on complaints about loud parties and eventually confiscate your stereo equipment if you don't turn down the sound. In some cities there exist what we call institutional mechanisms (that is, organisations specially designed for this purpose), which are in effect neighbourhood conflict-resolution centres —neighbours in dispute meet with a trained negotiator, who attempts to resolve the conflict. It seems inevitable that as population densities continue to increase, regulation over disturbing the privacy of others will also continue to rise.

Another example is the festival of Halloween. Processes of globalisation have meant that the festival is 'catching on' in Australasia, but there is a long way to go before it is celebrated with what can only be described as the fervour of North Americans. A contradiction has developed between the traditional and the modern with the rituals involved in the observance of this children's festival. The rituals require children to engage in behaviours which normally they are taught not to do. 'Trick or treating' involves going out in the dark, accepting gifts from strangers and, generally, in the name of 'fun', celebrating aspects of the supernatural that are in some respects at least inimical to established religions.

Or take tourism. As a source of revenue, tourism has become increasingly important for many countries starved of hard currency or undergoing transformation of their traditional income sources. Revenue from tourism throughout the world is now many billions of dollars each year, yet tourist preferences are fickle—a fashionable destination one year may not be popular the next. The Indonesian island of Bali since the October 2002 bombing (tourists are slowly returning to this favourite spot) is a good example of a once-popular tourist destination that is suffering from an unforeseen downturn, as are many Asian countries in the wake of events such as terrorist bombings in Indonesia, the SARS epidemic of 2003, and ongoing political unrest in Thailand. The tourist *gaze* (or way of looking) involves a search for authenticity, which is why 'undiscovered' locations are favoured (see Urry, 1990). As these places become fashionable, the paradox is that the authenticity is likely to be compromised by the increased numbers of visitors wanting to share the 'authentic' experience, especially as the local people become organised to take advantage of the income possibilities that tourism brings. Trekking in Nepal is an example that comes to mind. Likewise, 'ecotourism':

the search for pristine natural environments, which is likely to place at risk the very rationale for people going there in the first place. Examples of this are the Great Barrier Reef or Uluru (Ayers Rock). In the latter case, for many tourists a visit to Central Australia is incomplete without an ascent of 'the Rock' itself, in spite of the large sign placed by the traditional Aboriginal owners at the base of the chained track, which asks visitors not to proceed. This, combined with regular accidents, deaths and other emergencies, has prompted the suggestion that the climb should be forbidden and the chain removed. Yet even the traditional owners recognise the contradiction by acknowledging the climb is part of the 'been there, done that' aspect of the tourist gaze which brings tourists (and their revenue) in the first place. Striking a balance between preservation of the environment and conservation of the species within it, and exploiting it for tourism as well as general development purposes, is a difficult task.

An associated issue is the example of the consequences of world population growth, now at the point where the on-going potential for undernourishment (if not starvation) is the lot of probably the majority of the world's people. Famines are now documented with such regularity that the visual impact of exposure to such scenes on our televisions has lost some of its dramatic effect. This situation occurs at a time when agricultural 'overproduction' in the developed world is a major source of concern, with primary producers struggling to survive in the face of these huge food surpluses. As well, over-nourishment and its consequences are major health problems facing developed countries including Australia and NZ, with a huge industry having grown up around assisting people in those countries to lose weight. To make sense of such a situation it is essential to have an understanding of issues of social structure which includes the power relations between countries of the world. Food is a commodity to be bought and sold. Apart from some gifts of food in the form of aid, the ability of a developing country to feed its people depends on its ability to pay for the commodities needed, or at least be given credit to do so.

Speaking of the paradoxes of food, a final example. On a trip to the 'Emerald Isle', a visitor learning about the terrible set of events that is usually known as the great Irish Famine of 1845–52 when potato crops failed, cannot help but be struck by a shocking and indeed in many respects appalling paradox. In the midst of the starvation that depopulated the Irish countryside as well as spurred outmigration to other countries such as the US, some of the produce of Irish land that would have saved many of the local inhabitants from starvation, was being exported to Britain by Anglo-Irish landowners. Such a paradox or contradiction can only be explained by referring to the Irish social structure of the time, especially the relative position in the social hierarchy (what sociologists usually call the class structure) of the Anglo-Irish landowners and the poverty-stricken, landless Irish populace (see O'Neill, 2009). So the landowners grew rich while the poor starved.

The notion of contradiction or paradox is an important one to the social sciences in general and sociology in particular. The paradoxes and contradictions involved in urban living, Halloween, ecotourism, overpopulation and food supply, illustrate the complex ways in which the individual and society are related.

society and the individual

The concern to link individual behaviour to its broader social context is the distinguishing feature of the sociological quest and an essential one in understanding the complexities of the social world in which we live. In particular, it enables us to understand and counter the trend towards individualism, which has become a prevalent feature of contemporary life in the developed world. This view has grown from a type of 'pop psychology' that has fuelled a preoccupation, even obsessive belief, in the ability of the study of the lives of individuals to provide a sufficient framework for understanding the complexities of human social life. Look in any bookshop at the number of books available promising self-awareness and self-help. Solutions to complex social problems are held to be found in individual actions which may derive from particular individual failings. Political life is held to be explainable only, or mainly, in terms of the behaviours and personalities of individual politicians. Human conflict is frequently held to be the result of poor socialisation or the impulses of individuals. (For a broader account of this phenomenon see Beck and Beck-Gernsheim, 2002.)

The consequences of rampant individualism are felt in a number of spheres in society. One is the vulgarisation of the concept of 'rights'. Any problem, any grievance, any failure to get satisfaction can be cast in the discourse of rights and become the subject of litigation. Such an emphasis on solving the tension between the individual and society in favour of the individual is antisocial, in the classic sense of tipping the balance too far in favour of the individual. Concern with individual rights is important but the tension between the individual and the collective cannot be resolved by a narcissistic overemphasis on the individual alone. Arguably, commitments to some notion of 'civic duty', to mutual respect and to responsibility to society are important if our lives are not to be made into survival courses and our cities into combat zones in a dog-eat-dog world.

The nineteenth-century sociologist Emile Durkheim coined the term *conscience collective* (i.e. collective consciousness) to refer to those aspects of living in group life that require surrendering aspects of individuality in the interests of social harmony and cohesion. Arguably this has declined as individualism has increased, so social order is undermined. Take, for example, how what is defined as 'acceptable' behaviour has changed in what is called the *normative expectations* of watching a movie at your local cinema complex. On recent visits all of the following were observed: loud mobile phone conversations, running discussions on the plot, a domestic dispute voiced in loud, heated whispers, the smell of takeaway food such as curries or pizzas which permeated the entire theatre, and patrons going in and out of the theatre several times during the screening. One polite request for others to remain quiet was met with the rejoinder that if that particular person wanted to watch it in silence why didn't they hire a DVD and watch it at home! It seems that public theatres have become an extension of people's living rooms and domestic life is carried on as it is in private!

In the economic sphere, free-market economic rationalists argue that the best interests of the society as a whole will be served by the individual and the unrestrained pursuit of self-interest with an absolute minimum of governmental intervention. In the case of free-market economic policies, as a United Nations report concluded, while it is clear these policies are capable of economic growth, 'it is far from clear they are capable of creating just, civilised and sustainable human societies'. This is the result of 'insufficient account being taken of the effects [of these policies] on the poor, the vulnerable and on the environment' (UNICEF, 1994). Recent experience of what has come to be known as the Global Financial Crisis would bear this out.

Individualism is a powerful example in modern life of what we call an *ideology*. An ideology can be defined as a set of ideas that justifies a course of action; that is, it acts to rationalise a course of action in the sense of underpinning a preferred explanation or understanding with the sense of right and propriety. The emphasis on individualism isolates the individual from their social context. This recalls the famous utterance by the former British prime minister, Margaret Thatcher, when challenged on the effects her government's policies were having on the social fabric of British society as a whole: 'There is no such thing as society'. Denying the relevance (or even existence) of community or society ignores, or at least gives inadequate attention to, the collective level of analysis, as though an individual can somehow exist apart from this wider societal context.

The whole is more than the sum of its parts. A football team can be no more thought of as just a group of individuals than a whole nation can be understood by the sum of the individuals that comprise it. This is to recall the catchcry of the coaches of sporting teams all across the globe, who in their half-time 'pep talks' remind players that 'there is no "I" in the word team'. The relationships between the individuals in either a football team or a nation are of great importance in adequately accounting for what is going on. In the case of the football team, also important are the club's traditions, the levels of authority and relations between captains, vice-captains and team members, the complex codes through which tactics are communicated, and so on. In the same way, poverty cannot be understood only as the failure of individuals; it must also be understood in the context of the overall distribution of wealth within and between societies, by reference to the structure of society.

The example of a professional sports team is an instructive one. The consequence of gradual inflation of the salaries paid to sportspeople at the highest level has meant that fortunes, by any standard, have been earned by a few extremely talented individuals, such as soccer player David Beckham. The difficult task for coaches (usually paid a fraction of what their players earn) is to mould these highly paid individuals into a team so that the team's, as well as the individual's, performance is maximised. Sporting folklore has it that a team of individuals will always beat individuals who make up a team. Sometimes, though, the 'me' concept gets in the way of the 'we' concept. A coach who keeps an expensive player sitting out of the game as a disciplinary measure for failing to maximise team performance is not likely to be popular with the club owners or the fans.

The contrast with the way in which the relationship between the individual and society is constructed in different countries is an instructive one. While in the West there are highly individualised notions of self, in Japanese society, for instance, the relationship between the individual and society is constructed quite differently (see Singer, 1993: 96–128; also Mouer and Sugimoto, 1986). The primary cultural emphasis on identification with the group means that the relationship between the individual and society is constructed much less as a tension or contradiction than in Western societies where individualism prevails. The individual is considered subservient to the group. The cultural values of loyalty and harmony within the group (family, company, etc.) draw on the traditions of Eastern thought (both Confucian and Buddhist).

The difference in the way sport is played in Japan and in other societies is instructive on this point. American baseball players, socialised in an individualistic style of team performance, have often had great difficulty adjusting to playing baseball in Japan. The Japanese goal is the concept of *wa;* putting team performance ahead of individual performance (see Whiting, 1979). This contradiction is nicely captured in the 1992 film *Mr Baseball,* about the difficulties experienced by an American baseball player (played by Tom Selleck) in adjusting to the game in another country.

This approach to social life, it should be said, also has drawbacks, such as the implications the pursuit of group aims has for the potential harming of outsiders. The important point is that there is nothing inevitable or 'natural' about the nature of group life and the place of the individual within it, rather they are the products of history and culture. The cross-cultural example, however, sheds light on the nature of so-called economic individualism, the free-market ideology which holds that the individual pursuit of economic gain is the most effective manner to allocate economic resources and that society cannot survive unless individuals aggressively pursue their own individual self-interest. The example of Japan, economically successful by any measure, would seem to be a powerful counter-example.

A simple instance of the consequences of such free-market ideology can be seen in the operation of the housing market, an area which, for most individuals, represents the largest investment made in a lifetime. The market determination of housing prices, based on buying at a lower price and benefiting from a rise in values by selling at a higher price, means that some areas have greater increases than others according to market demand. In some of the larger cities in the world, huge rises in the price of houses have reduced affordability, not only for younger people trying to enter the housing market, but also for many members of occupations on which the rest of society relies for basic services, such as police, fire, health and postal services. Postal workers in London went on strike in an attempt to secure a 'London allowance' (in the form of extra pay) to enable them to afford London housing prices, and thus continue to provide the basic infrastructure of services that city requires. Already such housing pressures are felt in Sydney and to some extent in Auckland, where house prices greatly exceed those elsewhere in their respective countries. In the Canberra region, many of the workers who provide the basic infrastructure of goods and services that the national capital requires choose, on economic grounds, to live over the New South Wales border in the town of Queanbeyan, where house prices are more affordable.

Another example, outlined previously, is occupational health and safety. For a long time the major explanation for the causes of what were called industrial 'accidents' was the notion of 'accident-proneness'. This concept is drawn from industrial psychology and fails to take into account the broader social causes of what should more properly be called 'industrial injuries'. These social causes include the nature of the work relationship itself, the frequent priority of production over safety considerations and the lack of adequate safety precautions (such as guards on machines). Yet the focus on the individual level without considering the broader group level of analysis effectively blamed the worker for the injuries received (for an extended analysis, see Quinlan and Bohle, 1991). Within the field of occupational health and safety is the example of the digging of trenches.

Many workers over the years have lost their lives by being buried in collapsing trenches. Digging trenches is a common part of construction work. It is inevitable that, due to soil and climate variations, some trenches will collapse from time to time unless precautions are taken. Cave-ins can thus hardly be called 'accidents' in the sense of unforeseen chance events. Yet the technology for avoiding cave-ins is fairly simple, in the form of shoring, where a steel frame fits down the sides of the trench around the place individuals are working; it can be moved by a crane as the workers move along the trench. This costs money, however, including the wages of the crane driver. In all, the personal troubles of being buried in a trench can only be understood at the wider public level of employer–employee relations. Likewise, individual suffering and deprivation of various sorts cannot be understood only as an accumulation of individual experiences, but must also involve locating those individual experiences in their social and structural context; something that is central to a sociological way of analysing the social world.

conclusion

This chapter addressed the question of what is unique about sociological explanation. It is the concern with the relationship between the individual and society in a manner seeking to locate the individual in the larger social scheme of things. Furthermore, locating the individual must take account of contradiction and paradox. While there are considerable areas of overlap with other pursuits and other social sciences, the distinctiveness of a sociological explanation lies in its focus on relating the individual level of social analysis to the collective or group level.

4 the sociological imagination

The basic concepts outlined in Chapter 2 are important to all sociologists: the distinction between sociological and social problems, between macro and micro sociology, between private troubles and public issues, between continuity and change, and the importance of reflexivity. Sociologists work with these basic sociological ideas by asking, and pursuing the answers to, a number of key questions: '*What's happening?*', '*Why?*', '*What are the consequences?*',' *How do you know?*' and '*How could it be otherwise?*'. The early sociologists, amongst them Durkheim, Marx and Weber, began to explore these concepts and questions and apply them to the societies in which they lived. Sociologists continue this project to this day, moulding and adapting these basic concepts and questions to their own version of sociology and to their ever-changing worlds.

One sociologist whose version of these questions has been particularly influential is C. Wright Mills. Writing in 1959, he gathered together these questions and concepts and labelled the perspective that uses them to view the world as 'the sociological imagination'. My interpretation of this perspective is that the quest for sociological understanding of the world involves invoking the sociological imagination as a form of consciousness for understanding social processes.

Here, and in the following chapters, this notion is developed in some detail by arguing for a number of sensibilities or components to the sociological imagination. *Sensibility*, in this instance, means a keen appreciation of, or consciousness about, aspects of explanation.

My starting point is with the work of the British sociologist Anthony Giddens (1983: 16), who interprets the sociological imagination as 'several related forms of sensibility indispensable to sociological analysis'. For him, the sociological quest for 'an understanding of the social world initiated by the contemporary industrial societies' can only be achieved by the exercise of these forms of sociological imagination. For Giddens, the exercise is threefold: historical, cultural and critical. To this schema I shall add a fourth dimension, that of structure. Sociological explanation is likely to be incomplete unless these four considerations are taken into account. This chapter will deal with the historical and cultural aspects, the next chapter with the structural and critical.

historical

Giddens (1983) argued that one consequence of the attempt to model sociology on the natural sciences and to uncover general laws of human behaviour has been the severing of sociology from history as the social processes have been isolated from their historical context. But the two are so closely intertwined as to be virtually indistinguishable. As Giddens (1983: 165–6) says:

> We have to grasp how history is made through the active involvements and struggles of human beings, and yet at the same time both forms those human beings and produces outcomes which they neither intend nor foresee. As a theoretical background to the social sciences, nothing is more vital.

In other words, because history has an enormous effect on who we are as individuals and societies, it must be integral to the study of sociology. Wright Mills (1959) has alternatively characterised the relationship between the individual and society as between biography and history, as well as the way these intersect within social structures. Where does this particular individual stand as part of this particular society in relation to history? Where do individuals, such as Nelson Mandela and Barack Obama, stand in relation to their particular societies at this point in history?

Like the discipline of history, sociology also attempts to gain some understanding and comprehension of societies that no longer exist. The origins of sociology lie in the attempt to come to terms with and understand the massive transformation in the social world that we generally call the advent of modernity. Arguably, the ongoing social changes that have occurred in the past two centuries are more profound and far-reaching than any that occurred over the previous 10 000 years.

Some sociologists (for example, Game, 1991) argue that the pace of social change has accelerated in the past decade or two, so that the state of society is now sufficiently different from that of even our parents; we live in a distinguishably new period of human history. We have moved from the period of modernity to that of *postmodernity*. These changes include a lack of permanence in people's lives as the old certainties by which people lived are swept away. While there was always a significant minority who were exceptions, these 'certainties' about the bulk of one's life included being married to one person, living in the same house for long periods and having long-term employment in one job. With this new period of insecurity has come the end of the notion of global narratives such as 'progress' as well as faith in the ability of science and technology to solve the problems we face (for a review of the debate see Turner, 1997).

Other sociologists argue, by contrast, that while there have been major changes in how people live their lives, these changes have not been so monumental as to justify designating a new historical epoch. Instead, there is enough similarity with previous times to justify the term 'late modernity' (see Giddens, 1983). Coming to terms with these changes requires a clear understanding of the historical aspects, the first element in a sociological imagination. Attempts to understand particular social phenomena are likely to be inadequate unless the historical aspects are considered.

Among these changes, those involving the use of technology are some of the most important. As Giddens (1983: 19) argues:

> The sheer scale and pervasive character of technological innovation is undeniably one of the distinctive features of the industrialised societies today. Closely connected to it is the decline of tradition, the foundation of day-to-day life in the local village community and important even in urban life in the pre-capitalist era. Tradition encapsulated the present in the past, and implied an experience of time distinct from that which predominates in contemporary Western societies . . .

A good example is the way time was experienced. Through most of human history, time has been measured by the rising and setting of the sun, with no differentiation of time into 'work time' and 'free time'. The earliest clocks had hour hands but no minute hands. Only with the advent of industrial capitalism was there a need to divide time into smaller and smaller units: first, minutes to allow for 'punching on' and 'punching off'; then seconds. Finally, fractions of seconds were used to measure and improve productivity by the use of the stopwatch in the hands of the modern 'time and motion' experts (see Thompson, 1967). The implications of the changes in time measurement for how society operates have been enormous. Sociologists studying an earlier period must therefore take into account that conceptions of time were very different.

Yet the way sociologists use historical evidence as part of the sociological imagination is somewhat different from the way it is used by many conventional historians. While it is difficult to generalise, many mainstream historians attempt to understand the past for its own sake. Engaging in historical research is often pursued as an end in itself. In sociology, the quest is to understand the present in terms of how it came to be. The past is studied not just for its own sake but for what it can tell us about the shape our current society takes. To understand some aspect of our society, we first need to study the past.

The 'facts' of what happened in the past are as important to sociologists as they are to conventional historians, but the use made of these facts is more often put in an interpretive context. All scholarship involves selectivity, and what facts are selected as relevant will depend on the purpose for which the research is being conducted. Sociologists more often consider the implications of these facts for modern-day life. In addition, many conventional historians take the view that their subject matter can only begin after some period of time has elapsed, often 50 years. Sociologists, in comparison, tend not to be bound by such restrictions and tend to study more recent historical events.

In this sense, historical sensibility is the background to all understanding if it is not to be what is called *ahistorical*. This term means failing to understand and take account of the historical context in explaining what has occurred. An example is the issue of the affordability of housing, especially in Australia's large cities. One real estate agent observed of Melbourne in 2003, 'A million dollars now buys a pleasant family home, in a pleasant street in a pleasant suburb and nothing more' (*The Sunday Age*, 24 August 2003). Clearly there were a number of factors at work in what came to be regarded as a sustained housing boom, including low interest rates, favourable tax advantages for investment housing in the form of negative gearing and a first home owners' scheme. Yet a historical perspective is important in understanding this phenomenon. Housing affordability has always been an issue for those at the bottom end of society and many have never been able to fulfil 'the Australian Dream' of owning their own house. What has occurred is the spreading of the affordability problem into the middle, often dual-income-earning sector of society. Furthermore, Australian and New Zealand societies are increasingly becoming polarised into what, for simplicities sake, can be called the 'haves' and the 'have-nots'. As the 'haves' increasingly use different schools, hospitals, roads (tollways), means of travel (not public transport) and pursue different leisure interests (boating, snow sports and rugby union), the suburbs are increasingly divided into desirable and less desirable. For many of those who are having difficulty getting into their own homes, this means not being able to afford housing in suburbs close to schools, work and so on, and in those in which many of them grew up.

Another example is the institution of marriage. It is quite common to hear the view expressed that with the high incidence of divorce and the number of couples living together in de facto relationships that 'marriage is going out of fashion'. The evidence shows, however, that such a view is ahistorical. While the proportion of people 'currently married' has declined since 1976, this is due partly to factors such as people delaying marriage until they are older.

According to the Australian Bureau of Statistics (ABS, 2001, 2009), the median age for men at marriage increased from 26 to 32 years and from 23 to 29 years for women in the nearly three decades from 1981 to 2008. As well, there were the people 'between marriages', that is, divorced at any point in time (see De Vaus and Wolcott, 1997: 13). Even though more than two out of every five marriages fail, most divorcees eventually remarry. Likewise, most couples in the de facto category eventually tie the knot. What has changed is not being married itself but, as indicated, the practice on the part of a significant proportion of the adult population of being married to one person 'till death do us part'. Indeed, we use the term 'serial monogamy' to refer to this phenomenon. The term 'monogamy' is used to mean the practice of one man marrying one woman. 'Serial' here means only one at a time, but a number of times in succession. In 1997, for instance, a third of all marriages were remarriages, and of these thirteen per cent were going around a third time, and one per cent a fourth time (ABS, 2000b).

A historical sensibility is important in analysing the historically high rate of marriage failure. Was there some golden age, from which we have retreated, when most marriages were happy? Or was life for most people sufficiently brutal and short that there was little opportunity to experience marital unhappiness? What has changed about the way our society is organised that would help explain why the incidence of marital failure has apparently dramatically increased?

A number of factors would seem relevant to explore. First, increased life expectancy has meant that couples have a longer time to be together. Silver and especially golden wedding anniversaries were uncommon until the second half of the twentieth century. Second, it might be argued that couples today are more isolated than before. In the past, where couples continued to live amongst kinsfolk, one's marital relationship might not have been the most important affective relationship (that is, where emotion is involved). If one's marital relationship was not particularly rewarding, one could look to other kinship relationships. With urbanisation and migration, as well as the fairly recent notion of marrying for love (what we call the ideology of 'love marriages'), couples are more isolated from kin and have come to rely more on their marital relationships to satisfy all their emotional needs than ever before. Third, the capacity of women to leave unhappy marriages and live independently has changed. Several factors are relevant here, including the enactment since the 1940s of social welfare legislation to provide state support for divorcees, better education for women, and the growth in labour force participation by women. Fourth, the adverse social reactions to divorce, what we call the negative sanctions, have declined over time. As divorce has become more common, 'divorcee' is no longer the stigmatised category that it was even twenty years ago. Another way of saying this is that breaking up is now a more socially acceptable means of resolving marital unhappiness. Previously couples stayed together 'for the sake of the children' or to keep up public appearances, but it is now more socially acceptable to separate. Based on socio-logical and psychological research, the view has also developed that it may be less harmful for children in the long run if unhappy parents do separate (see Amato, 1993).

Another example of the importance of a historical sensibility might be the current culturally approved body shape, particularly for women, but also for men. A walk through any art gallery shows that the current fashionable body shape with its emphasis on slenderness is only of recent origin. Art gallery walls are adorned with paintings of fuller, hourglass figures for women (painted by artists such as Botticelli); figures once considered beautiful but now considered fat. Body shaping is now a massive industry in many countries; indeed, one of the features of late modernity is claimed to be that the body has become a project to be worked on rather than something to have or occupy (see Shilling, 2003). It is worked on by dieting, surgical alterations, injections, implants, hair-dyeing, shaving, waxing, piercing, plucking, tattooing, building-up, exercising and so on. All are designed to achieve a figure that is currently defined as fashionable and beautiful. A historical perspective on body shapes is therefore important. It allows us to challenge the belief that what is currently fashionable, including slimness, is somehow more 'natural'.

A historical awareness also helps us to make sense of new developments in the way our society is organised. An example is the phenomenon of 'mature-age mothers'. In Australia, the median age (the age at which half the women are older and half younger) for married women having their first babies has been steadily increasing from 23 in 1966 to nearly 31 in 2005 (De Vaus and Wolcott, 1997: 50; ABS, 2002, 2007). Births to mothers over 40 years were once rare (0.8 per cent of all births in 1980) but in 2002 the rate had increased to 2.6 per cent as a proportion of all births (ABS, 2003). By 2005, 52 per cent of all births were to mothers over the age of 30 years, up from 43 per cent in 1995 (ABS, 2007). A significant number of women, particularly those with higher levels of education, are delaying parturition (having babies) until they are well into their mid-to-late 30s. This phenomenon is historically new and not well understood. A sociological perspective on these changes is likely to contribute to an understanding of them.

A mature-age mother I know reports that, much to her consternation, she is sometimes mistaken for her children's grandmother rather than their mother. In seeking an explanation for such a development in the manner in which reproduction is organised, some historical sensitivity is important. Two factors seem relevant. First the trend is associated with improvements in contraceptive technology that makes planning to delay parenthood possible. Unreliable contraceptive technology in the past meant that sexually active women could probably not delay parenthood even if they wanted to. In other words, contraception has created the possibility of a much more deliberate choice of when to start a family. Improved contraception provides the means but not the rationale for delaying parturition. It is what we call a *necessary but not a sufficient* cause or explanation for mature-age mothers. Better contraception (particularly the pill) is a necessary part of the decision to delay having a family, but it is not a sufficient explanation by itself. We must also take into account women's growing participation in the labour force, a feature of the work scene for several decades now.

Mature-age mothers are often those who, understanding the disruption to a career that having a baby entails, have delayed a family until they are well established in the workforce. Alternatively, economic circumstances may require women to be in paid employment as long as possible to make substantial inroads into paying off a mortgage before leaving the paid workforce or going over to part-time work. A sociological analysis of such a phenomenon as mature-age mothers requires an understanding of this historical context. It is only by using a historical sensibility, for instance, that we can begin to evaluate the implications of the passage of paid maternity leave through the Australian Federal Parliament in 2010.

What a historical perspective 'tells' us is the subject of considerable debate. Indeed, we may construct some aspects of our histories to relate to modern times. For example, Japanese school children learn a very different version of that set of events we call the Second World War from that learned in Australia or New Zealand. So the uses of history are sometimes controversial, but a historical sensibility is important to a sociological imagination.

cultural

The second component of a sociological imagination is a sensibility to the cultural aspects of explanation. *Culture* is one of the central concepts of the discipline of sociology, as it is for anthropology. In these disciplines, however, the term 'culture' is not used in its conventional sense as something equivalent to civilisation or the 'higher' forms of artistic expression, such as classical music and opera. Rather, it is used to refer to the non-biological aspects of society, all those things which are learnt or are symbolic, including convention, custom and language. Together these components distinguish human behaviour and society from that of other primates. Culture includes such features as beliefs, values, ways of life and customary ways of doing things.

The scholarly discipline that takes the concept of culture as its central organising principle is anthropology; not only in its more traditional form of the study of non-Western tribal societies but also, most recently, in its focus on aspects of industrial society. Yet a cultural sensitivity has also been a feature of the sociological imagination since the earliest days of the discipline of sociology. The cultivation of cultural insights is important to the quest for a sociological understanding for two main reasons. One is to push back what is frequently the conventionally held notion of the boundary between the natural and the social world. The other is to challenge notions that some cultures are superior to others.

The question of the boundary between the natural and the social world is of major intellectual importance. Some disciplines, such as psychology, devote much of their energy to elucidating this boundary. The particular importance of a cultural perspective is to reveal, as several decades of anthropological research has done, the range and diversity of the means of human existence that have been followed in human societies, such that it is difficult with any certainty to say what is 'natural' or 'normal' for human society. Rather, we can talk about culturally specific forms that particular societies adopt. An example is mate selection. In Western society, monogamy (the coupling of one woman with one man) is the conventional social arrangement under which reproduction occurs. Yet anthropological evidence shows that virtually any combination of partners you can think of in terms of numbers of men and women are to be found in other societies (see Burns et al., 1983). To say that monogamy is the natural social arrangement is clearly non-sociological. Likewise, the current cultural pattern for mate selection in Australasia is through 'love marriages'; a supposedly free choice of partners. Yet as Berger (1963: 101–7) has argued, Cupid's arrows are often carefully aimed with the help of parents through such strategies as selection of schools and the encouragement of certain leisure activities. Many other cultures favour arranged marriages, where parents select the mate, usually on the grounds of some perceived compatibility. One system is not more natural than the other, nor should it be assumed that love marriages are superior to arranged marriages; the divorce rate attests to that fallacy.

It is this debunking of commonsense understandings of how society works that has been the role of traditional anthropology. One influential American anthropologist, Margaret Mead (1901–78), lived in Samoa during 1925–6, where she studied and wrote a controversial work (published in 1930) about the experience of growing up in that society, especially for young women. Her purpose was to hold up a mirror to North

American society of the time. This society was, in her view, obsessed with the 'problems' of that span of the life cycle called 'adolescence' or 'youth'. In her mirror, she hoped Americans might see their own concerns reflected. Understanding how very differently Samoan young people experienced that span of the life cycle brought into question much of the way in which the debates about young people in the United States were couched in terms of what was 'natural' or not.

Along with an awareness of the variety of forms of human organisation possible is the second component of a cultural sensibility—the dispelling of what is called *ethnocentrism*. The quest for a sociological understanding involves the task of overcoming a position that assumes one's own culture is superior to others and the standard against which others should be measured. *Racism*, the belief that one's own race or ethnic group is superior to others, is the most common expression of ethnocentrism. Of course, both racism and ethnocentrism have been potent forces in shaping world history. Their legacy has been slavery, genocide, ethnic cleansing and apartheid. Indeed, some of the worst atrocities have been perpetrated by one set of people against others on the basis of a claim that the race of the oppressors was superior. As Giddens (1983: 23) argues, ethnocentrism is deeply entrenched in Western culture, though it is also found in many (if not most) other cultures. He argues it is a challenge to:

> . . . break away from the belief, implicit or explicit, that the modes of life which have developed in the West are somehow superior to those of other cultures. Such a belief is encouraged by the very spread of Western capitalism itself, which has set in motion a train of events that has corroded or destroyed most other cultures with which it has come into contact.

An example is how marital unhappiness, a source of divorce in our society, is dealt with in other cultures. We can now add a cultural sensibility to the historical awareness of this question, which was developed earlier in the chapter. As the travel writer Paul Theroux (1992: 589) said in his observations of the Cook Islands after paddling around the Pacific for some months:

> Marriage was seldom stressful because the family was usually so supportive—the husband had his male friends, the wife had her female friends, the children were raised by all these aunties and uncles. When a marriage was seemingly that complex and casual, divorce was somewhat irrelevant. And lots of people stayed married by having absolutely nothing to do with each other—by rarely being in contact.

In other words, it is somewhat ethnocentric to assume that divorce is the only solution to marital unhappiness!

Avoiding ethnocentrism in the quest for sociological understanding involves an awareness of *cultural relativity*; that cultures do not exist on a hierarchy from better to worse. Rather, cultures are different so one cannot judge the cultural practices of other cultures by their own notions of what is appropriate behaviour. What can seem a normal practice in one country can seem very unusual in another. A nice example is Dutch windows. In Anglo-Celtic culture, notions of privacy and the distinction between public and private space are such that at nightfall it is usually considered culturally appropriate to draw the curtains or blinds over domestic windows; in other words, to mark off what occurs within the living spaces of private dwellings as private in the sense of removed from public gaze. A visitor to the Netherlands is therefore likely to be struck by the observance of a different cultural tradition, that of leaving downstairs windows uncovered at dusk to permit, indeed even encourage passers-by to observe the, most often, beautifully decorated interiors as well as families going about their daily lives (see Vera, 1989). Indeed, a visitor is likely to feel somewhat uncomfortable (something akin to a peeping Tom) at observing these rituals of daily life that are considered private in other cultures.

From the point of view of many Asians, the cultural practice in most Australian and New Zealand households of wearing shoes inside domestic dwellings is inappropriate on the grounds of cleanliness and hygiene. Likewise, the response to hot summer temperatures in this part of the world is to strip off to shorts and brief swimming costumes. In Arab countries, the response is to cover up, including head covers. In the light of concerns about the increasing rates of skin cancers, it is difficult to avoid the conclusion that the latter response is more appropriate.

Food preferences and habits are another good example of the need for a cultural sensibility. Anglo-Celtic culture has a relatively narrow definition of what is culturally acceptable to eat. Many Australians, for instance, cannot conceive of eating kangaroo meat, although on health grounds it is highly desirable, being very low in fat. Other European cultures, such as the French, tend to have a much less rigid definition of what constitutes 'offal' than the English. Animal body organs, such as brains, kidneys and livers, regularly appear on menus in France. Asian cultures are different again.

A woman of Filipino ethnic background lives in my suburb. She wears a pendant around her neck, which is very precious to her. It was made from her grandfather's thighbone. I have heard locals refer to this practice as 'bizarre'. We often have no difficulty labelling customs in other cultures pejoratively but have difficulty recognising the same in our own. The wearing of lucky charms in other cultures might be dismissed as superstitious, yet some aspects of custom in our own might also be considered to have the status of lucky charms. One is the common sight of cyclists riding along with their protective bike helmets not on their heads, but strung over the handlebars. Beliefs in its powers as a lucky charm to keep the cyclist safe seems the obvious explanation! Another is the practice of hanging St Christopher icons from car rear-vision mirrors, an attempt to ward off accidents, even by some considerably lapsed or non-Catholics. A cultural sensibility would recognise that a St Christopher pendant is no more 'civilised' or 'natural' than the thighbone of a loved one.

At the same time, questioning the limits to cultural relativity is important and very much part of exercising a sociological imagination through a cultural sensibility. On these grounds it may be necessary and indeed appropriate to argue that some things that other people do cannot be legitimatised on the grounds of cultural relativity. An example is the different positions occupied by women cross-culturally. Some cultures are what we call highly *patriarchal*, that is, experience a system of power relations organised in such a manner that men benefit the most. In some places, the position of women, who are exploited and repressed, is legitimatised by major belief systems. In some countries in the Middle East, women are not allowed by law to hold a driver's licence. Special exemptions had to be made for female American soldiers during the Gulf War in 1991 so they could drive military vehicles during the conflict.

An issue debated often in recent years is the cultural practice of 'circumcising' baby girls, which continues to be done by some migrants, particularly those of African origin, even after their arrival in Australia. The practice involves the removal of parts of the external genitals, especially the clitoris. Its purpose is reported to be the control of female sexuality, since the operation allegedly deadens sexual sensation and therefore is supposed to make the women less tempted into extramarital sexual relationships (see Armstrong, 1991). The issue is the degree to which cultural relativity should be extended before the practice is defined as 'mutilation', or an 'assault', and therefore incorporated under the definition of 'child abuse'. If defined as child abuse, should it warrant the attention of policing authorities and child protection legislation (see Family Law Council, 1994)? The question has increasingly been cast in a human rights language framework or *discourse*: are there fundamental human rights (such as not having genitals 'altered') which override cultural expectations? Are human rights absolute or culturally relative?

Yet even in this instance where condemnation has been widespread, issues of cultural sensitivity and relativity are relevant, particularly in deciding how best to bring about the cessation of the practice. If genital mutilation is the answer, what is the question? Are there alternate, more socially acceptable means of answering that question? For one thing, it must be seen in the context of social pressure on mothers to conform to cultural expectations to help assure their daughter's future marriageability. We might then seek to address other, more acceptable means of bringing about a desired end result.

If condemning such a practice outright, perhaps it is also necessary to consider cultural practices in the wider community, for instance, that of male circumcision. If removing part of the genitalia of baby girls is mutilation, why does the same standard not apply to removal of part of the genitalia of baby boys? There is similarly no medical justification. Yet attempts to have the surgical procedure 'chopped off' the list of operations for which part of the payment to surgeons is claimable from the public purse (on the grounds that it was a type of cosmetic surgery) led to a public outcry and a hasty backdown by the Australian government.

Furthermore, a historical sensitivity is also important. It is perhaps not widely known that clitoridectomies (the operation to remove the clitoris) were performed on adult women psychiatric patients in the nineteenth and early-twentieth centuries in developed countries such as the United States (Barker-Benfield, 1972). The purpose of the procedure then was also to make the women more 'manageable'. From a particular moral point of view, condemnation may be right and proper, but a cultural sensitivity arising out of a sense of cultural relativity is also important to the sociological imagination.

A sensitivity to cultural difference is a crucial component of the sociological imagination. Cultural difference can operate at a number of levels. The usual commonsense understanding is the *intersocietal* level; that is, between different societies. Here the effect of a sociological imagination can be powerful. It can introduce a new level of understanding about aspects of our society that are assumed to be a natural part of the human condition but which are, in fact, culturally constructed. A good example is the practice of 'burping babies' to bring up their 'wind'. As Hugh Jolly writes in his book of advice for new parents (1983: 69):

It would be interesting to discover when the emphasis on bringing up the baby's wind first began. The importance of 'winding' the baby has certainly been strongly emphasised in this country [United Kingdom] since Victorian times and in America, the need to 'burp' or 'bubble' the baby is similarly advocated. But this attitude to wind is by no means universal. It is not a feature of native mothercraft in developing countries, although it is now practised by the educated classes in such countries. Even in developed countries it is not a universal practice: a Czechoslovakian lady married to an Englishman had her first baby in England and was duly taught the ritual of winding the baby. She had her second child in Czechoslovakia, *where they don't have 'wind'*, so that when, in the hospital, she began to rub and pat the new baby's back to get up the wind, the doctors, nurses and mothers all asked her what on earth she was doing to her baby. [emphasis added]

In sociological terms, what is occurring is that the meaning of burps in babies is socially constructed in different ways in different cultures. In the former Czechoslovakia it had one meaning, while in England it had a quite different meaning. No meaning is more 'natural' or 'normal' than another.

At the intersocietal level (between societies), cultural differences are important in explaining how different societies develop. This can occur at either a micro level, involving some small aspect of the society, or at the macro level, between societies as a whole.

To the rest of the world, Australia and New Zealand are assumed to be largely identical societies sharing a history and a geography that casts them in a sort of sibling relationship, if at times a testy one, especially when sports is involved. Yet many cultural differences between the two societies exist—a phenomenon that often surprises Australian tourists when they visit Aotearoa for the first time. Many Australians reacted with amazement at the decision taken by the New Zealand government in the mid-1980s, with widespread public support, to ban visits by American nuclear powered and armed ships. The difference is in a major way a cultural one (albeit with a historical dimension). An important feature of what might broadly be called Australian culture (arguably much more so than in New Zealand) has been a sense of geographical and strategic vulnerability. This view was exacerbated by the experience during the Second World War of the bombing of Darwin. An unwillingness to risk offending our powerful and protective friends by, for instance, having the effrontery to ask whether their ships are nuclear powered or armed, is a much more important consideration for Australians than it has been for New Zealanders.

With migration being such a large feature of the modern world, a sensitivity to cultural difference is important to the sociological imagination within societies at the *intrasocietal* level (within the same society). One example of cultural difference is the attitude towards privacy that is espoused by members of different social classes. This is concretely reflected in larger cities in Australasia in the use of fences around property. From the 1950s onwards a process of *gentrification* of the inner-city suburbs in most of the larger cities occurred. Prior to that time, the inner city had been the preserve of working-class communities. After that time, living close to the centre of the city began to be attractive to younger, more affluent middle-class couples who bought up the inner-city housing and began to renovate it. Often one of the first items to be added was a high front fence. The cultural clash the practice created meant the newcomers were frequently criticised. Take a drive through the wealthy and poorer sections of your city and compare the fences. In many of the wealthy suburbs, the houses are like Fort Knox; the gardens and house are only glimpsed at from the road. Neighbourhood Watch in these suburbs must be impossible. That seems why, for Australians used to living in the state capitals, a visit to Canberra with its almost total absence of any front fences in most suburbs is so striking and almost a challenge to one's sense of what is normal.

Another example is beach behaviour. In the major cities on the coastline of Australia, different beaches attain quite different characteristics, which is nicely captured in a classic essay by Graham Little (1974). What you are likely to see on Sydney beaches on a fine summer's day will vary greatly between Bondi, Palm Beach and Lady Jane Beach. Likewise, on Victorian beaches very different patterns of enjoying the beach will be evident—compare Portsea or Lorne with Elwood or Middle Park beaches. So the notion of cultural sensitivity extends to aspects within a society as well.

A final example is the recycling of water. In the era of climate change, with gradual global warming and the drying of the climate in many parts of the world, water is becoming a more precious resource than ever before. Thus, culturally, we are beginning to value water more. There are observable cultural changes. Firstly there is the minimisation of water usage through such practices as installing dual-flush toilets and water-efficient shower heads, personal-hygiene practices (e.g. turning the tap off while brushing teeth), waterless public urinals, composting toilets and following the adage in relation to toilet flushing: 'if it's yellow let it mellow; if it's brown flush it down!'. Another move is towards the recycling and reuse of water; separation into greywater that can be used again and blackwater that cannot. In many societies this shortage has led to recycled water being put back into the drinking supply after treatment. Many cities are now heavily dependent on recycled water for the domestic water supply of their citizens. In one of the leading cities in the world, and the venue for the 2012 Olympic games, by the time Londoners pour themselves a glass of tap water it is estimated to have already been through the kidneys of nine others!

Yet suggestions that it occur in the Australian context have been firmly rejected. A referendum in 2006 in the Queensland regional city of Toowoomba rejected a plan to introduce a portion of recycled water into the town supply with a vote of 62 per cent against the water plan (*Brisbane Courier Mail*, 29 July 2006).

At the same time, talking about the culture of a society is not to assume that everyone in a particular society shares a particular culture. Indeed, sociologists have found it useful to talk about the idea of *dominant cultures* and *subcultures*. For example, male dominance or patriarchy has been, to a greater or lesser extent, an aspect of the dominant culture in many societies, but it is a dominance of heterosexual preference. Homosexual men have constituted a significant subculture in many societies. Likewise, cultural expectations are not uniformly adhered to. Not all Muslims approved of the death sentence passed on the British author Salman Rushdie any more than all Australians approve of the presence of American intelligence facilities on Australian soil, or all New Zealanders approve of the ban on nuclear ships. So cultural sensitivity and an awareness of cultural difference are essential components in the sociological quest if ethnocentrism is to be avoided.

historical and cultural considerations together

A sensibility to, and awareness of, both historical and cultural aspects is important in a practical respect for the sociological imagination as it enables us to understand societies for their uniqueness. A historical and cultural sensitivity, furthermore, can act as a sort of sociological bulsh[1] detector. It provides a means of questioning the historical and cultural context of statements. It should alert us, for instance, when we hear statements to the effect that 'marriage is going out of fashion' in its historical sense, or that slenderness is somehow more 'natural'. Likewise, when we hear statements such as, 'It's only natural for little girls to wear pink', we learn that it is nothing of the sort; it is a cultural convention for differentiating the sexes by the colour of their clothes or room paint.

By way of illustrating further how these components of the sociological imagination operate together, consider the question of how we are or should be responding to the threat posed by the HIV/AIDS pandemic. This threat came into a world where it was assumed that large-scale pandemics were a thing of the past and are now found only in less-developed countries. In the current absence of a cure for the diseases that are the result of the damage to the body's immune system caused by AIDS, prevention is the best strategy for limiting and ultimately controlling the pandemic. We know enough about the mode of transmission of the virus in bodily fluids to know that certain sexual practices, such as unprotected sexual intercourse with multiple partners, is highly dangerous; hence the promotion of safe sex with the use of condoms. To maximise the effectiveness of the health education funds spent on encouraging people to practise safe sex, it has been extremely relevant to know which practices are most dangerous in terms of transmission of the virus. Large-scale surveys of the sexual practices of the population have been needed to effectively target spending for maximum effectiveness. However, because of the private nature of this information, little has been available until recently. Researchers have had to rely on classic studies done in the past, such as the work of Alfred Kinsey and associates. Their pioneering and important work was published in 1948 in a book titled *Sexual Behavior in the Human Male*, followed in 1953 by *Sexual Behavior in the Human Female*. The application of a sociological imagination in order to understand the relevance of these classic works is important, especially given their overly grandiose titles.

The research surveyed sexual behaviour at a particular historical time (the 1940s), and culturally it surveyed a particular society (the United States). Applying a sociological imagination, the books should more appropriately be called *Sexual Behaviour in the American Male and Female in the 1940s.* The practical point is that the usefulness of this pioneering research for designing health education and prevention programs today is very limited. For this reason, health authorities, in most Western countries at least, have been conducting large-scale surveys of the sexual practices of their populations in order to design effective prevention programs and to target those groups who may be most at risk. The Australian research conducted by the Australian Research Centre in Sex, Health and Society at La Trobe University was published in mid-2003 in *Australian and New Zealand Journal of Public Health* (De Visser et al., 2003). Their research and that done in other countries (see Laumann et al., 1994) has changed many of the assumptions about sexual behaviour based on the Kinsey research. Higher rates of marital fidelity, and lower rates of homosexual experience were apparent today than Kinsey found 40 years previously. The passing of time, broader and more culturally diverse societies, and probably, most significantly, a better methodological strategy (that is, the means of conducting the research) all go towards explaining these differences.

Another example of how historical and cultural sensibilities operate together is the notion of sacred sites in modern society. Historically, because of their strong cultural associations to the land, most Indigenous cultures had and continue to have well-known sacred sites; that is, important spiritual places. Indeed, some of the major political struggles by Indigenous peoples have been to preserve and protect these sites, such as the sign at the start of the popular climbing route at the base of Uluru (Ayers Rock), placed there by the traditional owners, asking visitors not to embark on the climb out of respect for its sacredness. What are the equivalents in secular industrialised societies? Churches (and especially cathedrals) are an obvious example but other institutions also become imbued with spiritual meaning. Attempts to build shrines to capitalism, such as casinos, have failed to ignite much response and appear to do little to satisfy needs for spiritual observance. Instead, what has become important are battle sites such as Gallipoli, where large amounts of the blood of young Australians and New Zealanders, as well as many Turks, of course, and those from other countries as well, was shed. Indeed, an interesting sociological phenomenon has been the growth of 'pilgrimage' like tourism, not only to the Dardenelles in Turkey but also the Kokoda Trail in Papua New Guinea and more recently the First World War battlefields of Flanders and France. In the United States, the Vietnam War Memorial in Washington increasingly has the character of a sacred site, something akin to those of Indigenous peoples. Other candidates for 'white fella' sacred sites might be sporting arenas, such as the Melbourne Cricket Ground! A historical and cultural sensitivity is important in developing an understanding of the meaning of these sites.

A final example of the use of both historical and cultural aspects to sociological imagination is the changing conventions regarding tobacco use in public places. A historical perspective, together with an understanding of cultural issues, provides an interesting sociological perspective on the issue. In many countries popular tourist attractions are the historical re-creations of towns from the past—old buildings, people dressing up in olden-day clothing, working at historical jobs, etc. A curiosity about how people lived in earlier times has meant that these attractions are frequently on the 'must-visit' list for tourists as well as school tours to give 'living-history' lessons. Sovereign Hill in Ballarat is an example. In the re-created public places of these towns, such as in the bars, there are often curious-looking receptacles that are likely to evoke questions from children as to what they were for. They are spittoons, for the use of patrons given to expectorating in public. Spitting as a public habit has now largely died out in Western countries (except on sporting fields), in part because of health concerns about the spread of diseases such as tuberculosis. As with the spittoons of the nineteenth century, so perhaps ashtrays of the twentieth will become historical relics—will children of the 21st century need to ask their parents what ashtrays were used for? Will visiting Vulcan archaeologists digging up ashtrays in the *Star Trek* era wonder what on earth they were used for?

conclusion

This chapter has considered the first two of the four components of a sociological imagination. Taking the two aspects of history and culture together is important, as Giddens (1983: 26) argues, because only with these two sensibilities in mind is it possible 'to break free from the straitjacket of thinking only in terms of the society we know in the here and now'. What we have today is the result, not of some preordained inevitable process of development, but of a consequence of history and culture resulting in the unique organisation of the particular society in which we live. Being historically and culturally aware, and avoiding being ahistorical or ethnocentric, are thus central components of a sociological imagination.

note

[1]**bulsh**: abbreviation for bullshit, meaning rubbish, nonsense. *The Australian National Dictionary*.

5 structure and critique

This chapter considers the remaining two sensibilities of the sociological imagination. Whereas the historical and cultural components outlined in the previous chapter were elements to be taken into account in the analysis of social phenomena, the structural and critical components considered in this chapter indicate more styles of analysis, or ways of approaching the analysis.

structural

Sociology is concerned with the relationship between the individual and society. This is a way of saying that, as a discipline, sociology is concerned with understanding the behaviour of individuals in the social context in which it occurs. To elucidate that social context, sociologists often employ the notion of social structure as a conceptual tool or heuristic (something which helps us with the analysis) device. These structures it should be remembered are not rigid and consensual—that is, everybody agrees this is what it should be like—but precarious and shifting. It is, after all is said and done, individuals that make structures and allow them to act as a source of constraint.

The quest for a sociological imagination involves

developing a structural sensibility along with the various other types outlined. In trying to understand the social world then, the social structure acts as a signpost to the sorts of questions to consider. As outlined earlier, the key sociological questions to ask are, 'What is it about the way our society is organised as a whole that would explain this phenomenon?', and, 'How does the structure of society affect the behaviour of the individuals within it?'. An example is that of mature-age mothers outlined earlier.

A structural sensibility leads us to consider whether all women are delaying having families well past the age when their mothers and grandmothers did, or some women more than others? If delayed parturition is associated throughout the developed world with the level of education, then clearly some groups more than others are making these decisions. The trend towards mature-age motherhood is more pronounced amongst some class and ethnic groups than amongst others. What is it about the way our society is organised that helps explain this phenomenon? In my view, it is a social structure related to gender as well as class and ethnicity, in which the consequences of opting out of the workforce are greater in some sectors of the workforce than others. Professional or managerial careers, in particular, being largely defined in patriarchal or male terms, have made young women wary of taking time out of the workforce to have babies because of the potential impact on their careers (sometimes referred to as the 'mummy track').

A useful conceptual distinction that will assist in making sense of this element of the sociological imagination is the distinction between *agency* and *structure*. Do the actions of individual human beings (agents) create social structure, or does social structure constrain and create the actions of individuals? We can think of both agency and structure as being important but neither being solely responsible for a social phenomenon. Rather, it is a question of the relative combination of agency and structural factors.

Consider, for instance, that set of historic events we call the Second World War. Would it have happened at all if one particular human being, Adolf Hitler, had never been born? Explanations that stress the agency end of the continuum would say, 'No'—the events that followed were a direct result of (the agency of) that particular historical person. Explanations that stress the structure end of the continuum would be likely to respond, 'Probably, yes'—if Adolf Hitler had not come along to exploit the particular set of historical circumstances that existed in Weimar Germany in the 1920s, then some other particular person would have played the historical role that Hitler did. Similarly, the Second World War can be understood in structural terms (especially in the Pacific theatre) as being akin to a trade war in which securing resources was important. Of course, adequate explanations of the Second World War require some elements of both structural and agency explanations.

Similarly, how are we to understand the remarkable and unprecedented event in Australia in mid-2010 of a first-term prime minister being deposed by his party to be replaced by his deputy who thereby became Australia's first female prime minister? What combination of agency issues (Julia Gillard's personality in particular) as against structural issues (a vitriolic campaign by the country's mining interests against a proposal to increase taxes), lead to the downfall of Kevin Rudd? Certainly the media have preferred explanations towards the agency end of the continuum. A more structural explanation would examine the then PM's lack of a factional base within the Australian Labor Party. It would also look at the ALP policies aggressively targeted by a business sector only too well aware of the precedent-setting influence this tax might have on the global operations of large multinational

mining companies if other sovereign countries were embold-
ened to follow suit.

Certainly a structural component of the sociological
imagination is necessary to balance the ways in which history
is sometimes taught in a 'great person' (or perhaps more
usually, 'great men') approach, as if agency was all that was
at work and the course of history could be predominantly
understood in terms of the personalities and motivations
of political and other leaders. The argument being made in
this book is for a position more on the structural side of the
continuum; that the operation of those particular historical
agents, important though their personalities were, can
only be adequately understood within a broader structural
context. It is not to argue that particular historical agents
were unimportant, but it is to argue for greater emphasis
on understanding the social context in which those events
occurred.

The debate is not just an academic one, it should be said,
but is relevant in understanding current political events.
Would the apartheid system in South Africa have ended if the
particular historical person Nelson Mandela had never been
born? To what extent has the post-apartheid reconstruction
of South Africa been dependent on the continued health and
survival of Nelson Mandela? Another example is the collapse
of the former Soviet Empire. In the turmoil and chaos that
enveloped what used to be called the Warsaw Bloc, the danger
has been that a political leader of Hitler's type may arise to
exploit the political and economic conditions that now exist
in those countries. This danger is made more poignant by
the existence of a huge arsenal of lethal nuclear weaponry.
Certainly some historical parallels between Germany under
the Weimar Republic and Eastern Europe today can be seen
in the emergence of an ultra-nationalist political movement.
What has been called the 'politics of protest' may result in

an authoritarian figure who offers a path forward, above politics and beyond the messy and frustrating constraints of constitutional government. Only an approach that considers the importance of structure would be capable of understanding this analogy.

In politics, a feature of elections in Australia during recent decades has been unprecedented swings in voter preferences, resulting in major changes in the political landscape. While the particular individuals standing for office were not unimportant, an adequate sociological understanding of these events requires a structural component to the analysis. That structural analysis answers the question, 'What is it about the way our society is organised that is resulting in these changes?'. The answer would go something like this. These elections reflected an unease and insecurity on the part of many voters about the rapid pace of social change. These tensions have been surfacing at the ballot box as processes of social change, which have been going on for decades, gradually transforming the society people have known and in which they have lived. The political consequences have been that people have been less 'rusted on' to a conventional way of voting and there has been more volatility in the electoral result. These changes, furthermore, have been felt in all Western democracies, including Great Britain, Canada and the United States.

The processes of social change, which are collectively known as *globalisation*, are associated with late capitalism. Economies and therefore societies are being transformed as they become more internationally based. The transformation is from a blue-collar economy—that is, where a substantial proportion of the population earn their livelihood from working in manufacturing—to an economy in which many of these jobs are disappearing and other economic activity, such as service industries, come to dominate. For individuals, many of the old certainties about life are swept away in the course of economic reform. Jobs that were once performed on a secure, full-time basis have now been replaced in the name of labour-market reform, with a large proportion of the population now earning their livelihoods from insecure, part-time, short-term jobs which bear little relation to the traditional notion of a 'career'. For many workers the dignity of retiring at the end of a long and worthwhile career is being replaced by the ignominy of being squeezed out, laid off and retrenched a decade or more earlier.

In such a situation, the 'politics of blame' focuses on migrants, on Indigenous peoples, on welfare and on crime. These economic forces are leading to the polarisation of society between rich and poor, and between rural and urban. The anxiety expressed by the decline of the old order, in spite of indications that the economies emerging from a decade of recession are reasonably robust, has been powerfully reflected at the ballot box. My point is that we do not get very far in our understanding of political events, such as elections, by focusing (as the media tends to do) overwhelmingly on personalities. While these are not unimportant, what is also needed is a more structurally based account of what is occurring in the larger society, which will help explain the relative political instability associated with big changes in the political landscape. The ability of politicians to shape the society they are elected to govern is declining as powerful economic decisions are made by others with influence and international borders come to have less relevance.

A structural sensibility, therefore, is a necessary component of the sociological imagination. It means going beyond the level of individuals to take account of the broader structural context of the way in which that society is organised. To develop further the previous AIDS example, one of the features of the pandemic has been that different countries are affected differently, some worse than others. African countries are among the worst affected. On every other continent, the number of people who have died or are infected with the HIV virus, which eventually leads to the onset of AIDS-related medical conditions and ultimately death, are measured in the thousands. In Africa, the number is measured in the millions. In 2008, sub-Saharan Africa was home to 67 per cent of all the people on the planet living with HIV and 71 per cent of those newly infected, and of all deaths from HIV/AIDS so far, 72 per cent have been in Africa (UNHIV/AIDS 2009). The toll of human suffering at an individual level is revealed by a couple of examples: a Kenyan grandmother struggles to bring up all 24 of her grandchildren as her own children as well as their spouses have died from the disease; a Zambian bank decided to include HIV testing in pre-employment medical examinations, only to abandon it when eleven of the first thirteen candidates tested positive (Hamblin, 1994: 71).

Why has this pandemic been so bad on that continent? In trying to understand why the progression is much worse there than in other parts of the world, a structural component to the explanation is necessary. Explanations that focus only on individual components do not go far enough. It is also necessary to take into account issues to do with the social structure and organisation of many African societies. Consider the boxed text from the AIDS Epidemic Update released by the UNAIDS agency in December 2002 (UNAIDS/WHO, 2002: 19).

In the developed world, the AIDS pandemic, now entering its third decade, is primarily a homosexual phenomenon associated in particular with unprotected sex. In the developing world, and in Africa in particular, the character of the pandemic is primarily heterosexual. It is both a sociological and a social problem with tragic

why do young African women appear so prone to HIV infection?

Despite recent positive trends among young people (especially females) in some African countries, overall about twice as many young women as men are infected in sub-Saharan Africa. In 2001, an estimated 6–11% of young women aged 15–24 were living with HIV/AIDS, compared to 3–6% of young men. This appears to be due to a combination of factors.

Women and girls are commonly discriminated against in terms of access to education, employment, credit, health care, land and inheritance. With the downward trend of many African economies increasing the ranks of people in poverty, relationships with men (casual or formalized through marriage) can serve as vital opportunities for financial and social security, or for satisfying material aspirations. Generally, older men are more likely to be able to offer such security. But, in areas where HIV/AIDS is widespread, they are also more likely to have become infected with HIV. The combination of dependence and subordination can make it very difficult for girls and women to demand safer sex (even from their husbands) or to end relationships that carry the threat of infection.

Studies have shown that young women tend to marry men several years older, and that their risk of infection increases if a husband is three or more years older than they are. Meanwhile, ignorance about sexual and reproductive health and HIV/AIDS is widespread. In countries with generalized epidemics in Africa, up to 80% of women aged 15–24 have been shown to lack sufficient knowledge about HIV/AIDS. This, combined with the fact that young women and girls are more biologically prone to infection (the cervix being susceptible to lesions), helps explain the large differences in HIV prevalence between girls and boys aged 15–19.

consequences. In order to begin to answer this social and sociological problem, reference to the structure of these societies is necessary. In particular, some reference to the structure of power relationships between men and women in which men dominate, *patriarchy*, is an essential starting point. To a much greater extent than their Western sisters, African women find it difficult to negotiate about sexuality, as is characteristic of a highly patriarchal society. As a result, HIV prevalence is higher among women than men at 60 per cent (UNHIV/AIDS, 2009). In one study 47 per cent of men and 40 per cent of women in Lesotho indicated that women have no right to refuse sex with their husbands or boyfriends (Andersson et al., 2007). In other words, social factors such as the relative powerlessness of women are important.

There are other social factors as well. Economic opportunities for people to gain livelihoods are structured in such a way that migration in search of work is a major feature of the pattern of life. Many people, particularly African men, must spend long periods away from their homes due to work activities. In such a context the usual constraints on multiple sexual partners are lessened and the likelihood of HIV transmission is much greater. In other words, the spread of the virus has less to do with the characteristics of individuals and more to do with the organisation of the society in which they live.

Failure to take adequate account of the structural level leads to a common way of thinking in our society, which the quest for sociological understanding attempts to overcome. Focusing only on the individual level of analysis to the exclusion of the structural level encourages a sort of rationale or justification for the social phenomena called the *ideology of victim blaming*. Victim blaming occurs when individuals themselves are held to be responsible for what happens to them. It fails to engage a structural sensibility to also help explain what occurs. An example is rape. While there has arguably been some change for the better in recent times, there is still often the assumption that the woman somehow deserved what happened to her. Either she was wearing clothes that from a male point of view could be defined as 'provocative', she was walking in a 'dangerous' place at an inappropriate time (late at night), she was assumed to have encouraged the man in such a way he was justified to interpret it as a 'come-on', or said, 'no' when he assumed she really meant, 'yes'. In other words, the victim is blamed for what occurred. This approach, still often seized upon by defence counsel as an appropriate line when defending charges of rape, pays inadequate attention to the structural context of patriarchal gender relations in this and other societies, or indeed the rights of women to wear what they want, go where they want or generally act as they want. In all, the victims are blamed for acting like autonomous, 'free' members of a society of which they comprise more than 50 per cent! Having a structural sensibility is therefore important to avoiding this sort of 'blaming the victim' response, which the lack of a sociological understanding often engenders.

Another example of blaming the victim was discussed in an earlier chapter in the example of health and safety at work. Explanations for what have traditionally been called 'industrial accidents' have usually been couched in terms of 'accident-proneness'. As was argued earlier, this explanation for what should be more appropriately called 'occupational injury' fails to take account of the structural context in which employer–employee relationships are constructed. One structural constraint of this relationship is the requirement that expensive machinery be operated on a 24-hour basis, making shift work necessary. Working at night under conditions akin to permanent jet lag predisposes workers to more injuries, proportionately speaking, than on day shifts. This is hardly surprising to anyone who has ever worked night shift when their body's circadian rhythms become out of kilter and they have difficulty getting adequate sleep in urban environments during the daytime. To blame workers for the injuries that occur is by no means the whole story and does not take adequate notice of the production relations under which employment occurs.

This is not to argue that the individual level of analysis has no bearing on understanding the phenomenon. Rather, it is to argue that we do not get very far in our analysis of society if we focus only on the individual level. This issue is tied up with the extent to which individuals are responsible for their own actions. Individual workers may be careless, or indeed stupid, resulting in injury to themselves or others at work. But that is not the whole story. The design of jobs for maximum productivity rather than any sense of job satisfaction or personal enrichment may lead to careless or silly behaviour out of extreme boredom. Furthermore, failing to observe safety procedures may not just be a matter of worker irresponsibility, but a quite reasonable response to a particular set of circumstances.

The wearing of ear muffs to minimise hearing loss when working in noisy environments is an example of the last point above. Quite apart from the fact that they represent fitting the worker to the job rather than vice versa (installing quieter machinery which would remove the need for ear muffs), their effectiveness is limited if one also wears spectacles, they are uncomfortable to wear in hot, humid environments, and they virtually prevent any communication between fellow workers (about the only thing that can lessen the boredom). There is also the infamous example of the Brisbane tree feller who was killed when his ear muffs prevented him hearing the shouted warnings of his workmates when a tree was about to fall on him. Or the tragedy of the four rail maintenance workers in Western Australia who were killed by an on-coming train when the combined effects of the noise of the jackhammers they were using and their ear muffs meant they failed to hear the warning signal from the train driver (Mathews, 1985: 111).

A feature of the structural component of a sociological imagination, therefore, is that we should be suspicious of explanations for social phenomena based on some notion of irrationality on the part of the people involved. Indeed, in the quest for sociological understanding of the social world, it is another component of our sociological bulsh detector. What may appear irrational at the level of the individual, may appear quite different when the wider social structural context is taken into account. Definitions of rationality, in fact, are often culturally bound.

We know that the best way both to avoid contracting the HIV virus at the individual level and of containing the pandemic at the societal level is by preventing the transmission of bodily fluids through safe-sex practices and by not sharing intravenous needles. The use of condoms and brand-new needles are the easiest and most effective means of doing this. Public health education campaigns have promoted the use of condoms, a simple device officially approved and heavily promoted in many societies today, even to the extent of placing vending machines in some high-school bathrooms. Much of the campaign, however, is aimed at overcoming the traditional male objection to wearing the device ('It's like showering in a raincoat', is often quoted) by encouraging women to persuade their male partners to wear them: 'Tell him, if it's not on, it's not on', or, 'No glove, no love', have been the favoured slogans. Yet we know that the campaign is not working very well. While condom sales have dramatically increased since the beginning of the pandemic and a wider range of condoms is now available (including ones that glow in the dark and others that are Vegemite flavoured!), surveys in a number of countries reveal the occurrence of a significant incidence of unsafe sex (see De Visser et al., 2003; Coggan et al., 1997).

Before we rush to blame the victims for being stupid enough not to use condoms, it is necessary to consider the wider social context in which sexuality occurs in our society. In particular, we need to consider the nature of gender relations, especially with the traditional expectations of male initiative in defining what will or will not happen. Condoms continue to be what sociologists call 'positioned' or located in a male discourse, as revealed, for instance, by the brand names under which the world's condoms continue to be sold: 'Sheik', 'Ramses', 'Trojan' or the even more bizarre 'Roughrider' are masculine examples, balanced by brand names such as 'Lifestyle' and 'Mentor' that have less connotations of gender. Product differentiation has also seen the reintroduction of condoms of different sizes but mindful of male discourse, attempts to buy size 'small' will be disappointed; instead, they are available in 'large', 'extra-large' and 'jumbo'!

So, in spite of condom vending machines being installed in women's toilets, and in spite of pretty little velvet holders being available so that when a woman accidentally drops her handbag in public she is not embarrassed by displaying her condoms, it is still difficult in terms of the social practice of femininity for women to follow the health injunction of 'not leaving home without one!' (see Willis, 1994).

A structural sensibility is important in understanding many aspects of society. One thing that bothers people today, for example, is the apparent decline in the quality of customer service in retailing. Shopping has become a major form of leisure activity, especially for women in affluent Western societies—aptly summed up by the phrase, 'shop till you drop' (see Prus and Dawson, 1991). Yet the enjoyment of this form of leisure is often diminished by what are considered to be the attitude problems of retailing staff: surly, indifferent and sullen, with not enough of them, especially in the large department and chain retailing stores. What was assumed to be some golden age of retailing service in the past has been replaced by self-service. A structural sensibility would indicate that to blame the employees alone for the decline in customer service is not the whole story, as many of the readers of this book who earn a part-time living in retailing will know only too well. Indeed, it has an element of 'blaming the victim' about it. The more structural explanation would focus on how, in an effort to improve their competitive position, retailers have moved to mass discount pricing.

In order to stay profitable with reduced margins, employers have sought to cut costs; especially labour costs. In other words, employers have sought to improve their competitive position at the expense of their workers. The result has not only been less full-time retailing jobs but also the creation of retailing jobs that involve part-time employment, increased workloads, few prospects for advancement, little job security and declining pay. Most jobs have been made more routine, involving lower skilled tasks such as cash register operation and shelf stocking. Lower staff training costs is the aim. In this situation the 'attitude' problems of retailing staff are perhaps more understandable. It is little wonder that service has declined.

A structural sensibility is also often crucial when attempting to understand major social problems. One of the foremost of these in the Australian context is the continued existence of a population enclave of the original Indigenous population, whose health and other living standards are akin to those of some of the poorest countries—in a country that otherwise prides itself on being one of the most developed in the world! For many white Australians, the most visible sign of this is drunkenness amongst the Indigenous population. Viewing such drunken behaviour is wont to bring out the latent racism that many white Australians harbour. Victim blaming appears quickly as an explanation for the behaviour observed. Yet a structural sensibility tells another story entirely.

Alcohol abuse is a major social problem in some Indigenous communities. Many have and are attempting to ban its sale within community boundaries. The 2007 intervention by the former federal Howard government was another broader attempt in this direction. Data collected on a national scale shows the extent of the problem in recent history. One estimate is that about five per cent of Indigenous women and 25 to 33 per cent of Indigenous men can be classified as heavy drinkers, compared with the white population—one per cent of women and five per cent of men. Among the Indigenous population, half of male deaths and a fifth of female deaths 'have alcohol listed as a cause on their death certificates' (Callan, 1986: 45). The burden of alcohol-related disease borne by Indigenous Australians is estimated to be almost double that of the general Australian population (Vos et al., 2007).

The damage to health is part of a health pattern seen most often in a third-world country, not a developed one. Life expectancy for Indigenous Australians is 59 years for males and 65 for females (ABS, 2006), about seventeen years less than that for white Australians. Infant mortality is three times the rate for white Australians. Tuberculosis, trachoma and leprosy, all found in Indigenous communities, are practically unknown amongst white Australians (Social Justice Collective, 1991: 209–10). Poor health status is both a feature and a result of a general malaise within Indigenous communities and it is also reflected in unemployment rates many times higher than those found in white communities.

Gaining an adequate understanding of this complex social problem requires analysing its roots, particularly the structural situation in which the Indigenous community finds itself. At the first level it is clear there are strong reasons for excessive alcohol consumption. Frequent drinking to excess is an understandable response to the structural location of Indigenous people in Australian society. The reasons include such social and psychological considerations as powerlessness, low status, lack of privilege as a minority group, inadequate housing and employment, boredom, loss of cultural identity, feelings of inferiority and frustration, loss of land rights, lack of pride, peer group pressure and reaction to racial prejudice. But developing a structural sensibility to the sociological imagination may require going to another level of analysis.

Indigenous people are often subject to relentless entre-preneurialism by whites who sell them the alcohol in a manner reminiscent of drug pushers. Furthermore, it is now well understood by many white Australians that in cultural terms, Indigenous Australians have a different relationship with the land to whites. For the Indigenous population, land was and is viewed in a spiritual, long-term manner; not in terms of economic rights (a resource to be bought and sold) but on a much broader base. The land bestows identity as well as provides social and spiritual rights for Indigenous people. There has been a gradual recognition of the adverse effects, including health effects, that the dispossession of land has on Indigenous communities. There has also been a growing awareness amongst white Australians about the centrality of ownership of land as a means for Indigenous communities to come to terms with living in contemporary Australian society. One of the consequences of a massive lack of cultural understanding of Indigenous people is alcohol abuse. The recognition has been reflected in the growth of the land rights movement as one important strategy for overcoming the social problems experienced. A similar social movement has been an important part of recent New Zealand history.

We should, however, be cautious about thinking we have come very far in this process of cultural understanding and reconciliation in spite of the dramatic apology in the Australian federal parliament by the then prime minister Kevin Rudd in February 2008. Only since the Mabo land rights decision in June 1992 have we begun to move beyond what has been the legal basis for the forcible white conquest of Australia, and an overturning of the idea that the land was *terra nullius* (not owned by anyone). Failure to even recognise the original Indigenous inhabitants as Australian citizens was something only rectified by the referendum of 1967 when Indigenous people were first counted in the official census. The path to reconciliation remains a difficult one and attempts to settle land claims made possible under the legislation arising out of the Mabo case remain highly contentious, especially in some states.

Likewise, courses in Australian history, at least until recently, only began with the arrival of Australia's first settlers, many of them reluctant, in 1788. The issue of whether the arrival of white settlers should be taught in school systems around the country as a 'settlement' or an 'invasion' is still a contentious one. The issue of a formal treaty with the Indigenous people, recognising their tenure of the land prior to white settlement, is still considered 'too hard' politically. With a structural sensibility, a link between the controversy over the Wik decision and subsequent attempts to extinguish native title to land, and the poor state of Indigenous health, should be obvious. Extinguishment in 1998 of the last vestiges of native title in the name of giving 'certainty' to pastoralists have only worsened Indigenous health problems, including those involving alcohol.

The contrast with the New Zealand situation is instructive. While considered only a beginning and in no way a panacea for ameliorating racial problems, the gradual legal recognition through the 1980s of the Treaty of Waitangi, first signed in 1840, has had symbolic and legal consequences in recognising the importance of land ownership to cultural identity (see Orange, 1989). It has also provided a basis upon which issues of disputed land ownership can be resolved through a special tribunal established for this express purpose. But even when governments have attempted to recognise the link between land and cultural identity, however symbolic, widespread racist attitudes on the part of the white population have sometimes stymied the attempts. Changing place names back to their original Indigenous names is one such example.

A decision taken in Victoria in 1991 to revert the name of the Grampians National Park in central Victoria to the original Indigenous name of Gariwerd met with a hostile response from some local white Australians, who threatened to tear down the signs announcing the name changes. An early decision by an incoming conservative state government in 1993 reversed the decision, ironically coinciding with the beginning of the International Year of Indigenous Peoples. In the New Zealand context, similar name changes have occurred with widespread local white opposition. For instance, when the decision was made to call that most beautiful of New Zealand mountains by its original Maori name, Mt Taranaki, instead of Mt Egmont, the name given to it by Captain James Cook after an English aristocrat. In the recent settlements of tribal land claims, one in the South Island will see the name of Aotearoa's highest mountain revert officially to Aorangi ('cloud piercer') instead of Mt Cook.

To recap, the argument being made is that an adequate understanding of the problem of alcohol abuse in Indigenous communities can only begin by considering the structural context of Indigenous people in a predominantly white Australian society. This does not make it less of a problem, it should be said, nor does it absolve Indigenous alcohol abusers from responsibility for the damage caused. What it does say, though, is that we will not get very far in our understanding of the problem, which is an essential precursor to trying to ameliorate the problem, if we remain only at the level of the individuals themselves. Our sociological bulsh detector should tell us that blaming or 'cracking down' on the abusers is not likely to get us very far.

A structural sensibility, along with the other components of a sociological imagination, is crucial in the quest for sociological understanding of the social world. It is an aspect of the sociological imagination that is sometimes misunderstood. These structures are not necessarily fixed, rigid and settled. Instead, they may be fluid, constantly evolving and contested. As outlined, when attempting to understand some aspects of the society in which we live, it is a way of orienting to a broader group level of analysis; of asking, 'What is it about the way our society is organised that results in this or that occurring?'. It is, as Berger (1963) argues, understanding the particular in terms of the general; how what happens to individuals can be 'made sense of' sociologically speaking in terms of what's happening in the society as a whole. When it happens to one person it is idiosyncratic and anecdotal. When it happens to lots of people in one society, such as to constitute a pattern or a regularity, then that's when sociologists get interested (indeed fascinated, some even excited!), especially if it gives some insight into what is happening to our society as a whole.

critical

The final component of a sociological imagination is the critical component. Here, it is important to note, the term 'critical' is being used somewhat differently from its common meaning of being negative about something. Rather, the term is used in sociology as being reflexive or sceptical about the social world, and of being engaged in a *critique* of the existing social world. A critical sensibility is implied, as outlined in Chapter 2, by the last two questions to be asked in trying to understand a particular social phenomenon from a sociological point of view: *'How do you know?'*, and, *'How could it be otherwise?'*.

Applying a critical sensibility means engaging in *systematic* doubt about accounts of the social world. Not all accounts of the social world are likely to be equally accurate, so the basis on which the quest for sociological understanding can proceed is that of scepticism about the claim of any statement to be a valid account of a particular matter. It is a way of proceeding which aims to narrow the range of doubt as much as possible. In exercising a critical sensibility, competing explanations for particular social phenomena are approached by trying to uncover and expose as many as possible of the ambiguities, misrepresentations, distortions and even falsehoods among those competing claims. It seeks to *demystify* these competing explanations by exposing them to systematic doubt.

A critical sensibility has two components. The first is common to all intellectual and scientific endeavour and concerns the use of evidence. Asking, *'How do you know?'* is a way of considering both, 'What's your evidence?', and, 'Is the claim you are making justified in the light of what we already know about the social world, or are you going beyond that?'. Being critical does not mean only being negative: it may eventually mean being positive about something. What it does mean is carefully considering the evidence that is available before deciding your position.

There is also a second level, more specific to the quest for sociological understanding of the social world, that of asking, *'How could it be otherwise?'*. Opposing the view that sociology can and should emulate the natural and physical sciences in its method of understanding the world, Giddens (1983: 26) states:

> No social processes are governed by unalterable laws. As human beings we are not condemned to be swept along by forces that have the inevitability of laws of nature. But this means we must be conscious of the *alternative futures* that are potentially open to us. [Here] the sociological imagination fuses with the task of sociology in contributing to *the critique of existing forms of society*. [emphasis in original]

As we have seen, sociology emerged in the nineteenth century as an attempt to understand the massive social changes brought about by the French and Industrial revolutions. This traditional focus remains central. As Tepperman (1994: vii) argues: 'Even today, sociology remains, at its core, a debate about the human ability to improve social life through reason and organised action'.

The sociological quest involves not only description and explanation to demonstrate what is, it also involves asking what *might be*. No particular vision of what might be is dictated by this application of the sociological imagination. Indeed, different sociologists will frequently have different recommendations of what should be done in a particular situation. It is the concern with critique itself that is a crucial aspect of the quest for sociological understanding. As Giddens (1983: 166) argues, 'As critical theory, sociology does not take the social world as given but poses the questions: what types of social change are feasible and desirable and how should we strive to achieve them?' This, he adds, is because sociology, along with the social sciences in general, 'is inherently and inescapably part of the subject matter it seeks to comprehend'.

The question of what alternative futures are possible and desirable inevitably raises questions of values and objectivity, which are present in all academic disciplines. Can the quest for sociological understanding be value-free? Can personal values and experiences be put aside when social phenomena are approached for study? Can *bias* (interpreting evidence according to one's values) be avoided? These questions have been the subject of considerable debate in the discipline.

It is now widely accepted that the sorts of values held by people in general, and therefore by social scientists such as sociologists as well, are bound to influence all that they think and feel and how they act. What topics are chosen for investigation, how those sociological problems are investigated, and what sort of conclusions are reached will all be influenced by personal values. The common position taken in the discipline today, following Gouldner (1973), is that the same critically reflexive approach to the study of social phenomena in general should also be applied to the question of values. In this book, for instance, the examples chosen to illustrate the argument reflect, to a certain extent, my interests and therefore my values. The fact that most of my teaching and research has been in that area of sociology called the sociology of health and illness means that a considerable proportion of the examples I have chosen come from that field.

Arguing this position on values is not to say that objectivity is not important. Rather, it is a recognition that it is necessary to work out when these values should be kept out of the teaching or research process (such as in the interpretation of research findings) and when they should be expressed, not attempting to be value-free. For instance, I have said in this book that female genital mutilation is outrageous and has no place in modern society. I have also said that men in particular, but also women, need to 'get their act together' in relation to practising safe sex, preventing the spread of the HIV virus further in the community. These are examples of my values and many readers may not agree with them. Expressing them here is not dictating to readers but challenging them to make up their own minds about the issues at hand.

My point is that saying what sorts of social change are desirable and feasible is very much a part of the sociological imagination. We might not agree, for instance, on the extent to which land rights will ameliorate the conditions of the original inhabitants of countries such as Australia and New Zealand, but discussing and arguing the issue is as much a part of the quest for sociological understanding as is the task of describing and explaining the situation. Indeed, Coulson and Riddell (1970: 86) go further and state, 'The claim that non-controversial value-free sociology can develop in a conflict based social structure is theoretically untenable, practically unrealistic and morally and politically disastrous'.

Critique is an important part of what sociologists do. It is this debunking or demystifying aspect of the sociological imagination that has given the discipline its somewhat controversial character. It arises from the tendency of sociologists, as part of the quest for sociological understanding, to challenge official explanations for things or to challenge those in authority who have a particular vested interest in reality being portrayed in a particular way. For example, it is both convenient and comfortable for rich people to believe they are overtaxed and that poverty no longer exists, so the amount of tax they pay appears excessive. A sociologist such as Phillip Raskall (1978) is not likely to be very popular, therefore, when he shows that high-income earners on the basis of published statistics actually pay a lower proportion of their income in tax than the rest of the population, and that the proportion of the total wealth of the country owned by the top few per cent of the population is actually increasing. The 30-year trend of rising inequality has continued with the richest boosting their share of Australian income significantly over the last five years in spite of the Global Financial Crisis. The top one per cent of taxpayers are the richest they've been, in relative terms, since the 1950s, even after the ravages of the GFC. (*The Sydney Morning Herald*, 10 April 2010). Based on data by Leigh and Atkinson (2010), analysis shows that the richest one per cent of taxpayers—those earning more than $197 000 a year—accounted for 9.8 per cent of all income in 2007–8. This was an increase on their 8.8 per cent share in 2002–3. This took the top one per cent of taxpayers' share of all income to its highest level since the 1950s (see also Atkinson and Leigh, 2005).

What sociologists say about any issue may cut across moral, political or religious beliefs. Indeed, when it is not assumed to be synonymous with socialism, sociology is sometimes accused of being inherently subversive. This is certainly not the case in the sense of promoting radical social change of a revolutionary nature, and generations of students who have come to the discipline expecting this have been sorely disappointed. Rather, the sensitivity to critique is to ask questions about what else is possible and not assume the current social organisation of society is somehow ordained or the only one.

It is, of course, not only sociology that experiences this controversial character. Any person or organisation seeking to understand how our society actually operates may experience it, even an official government body. An insight into this process was reported by the ABS (1993), an official governmental body whose job it is to collect information about how Australian society is changing, so that it provides the basis for the provision of services such as for the elderly. The report, termed a 'Social Atlas', documented the enormous inequalities that exist between different parts of Melbourne, in particular between eastern and western areas. On the release of this report, a Victorian cabinet minister of conservative persuasion was heard to opine that while he welcomed the release of the report as useful for planning purposes, he did not see it as 'helpful' for Melbourne to see itself as polarised (*The Age*, 23 December 1993). To which the critical sensibility question has to be, 'Helpful to whom?' To the residents of these suburbs whose resources, services or whatever are lacking compared with other parts of the city?

The debunking and demystification that is so much a part of the sociological imagination is concerned with challenging the myths or ideologies by which society operates. An example is the so-called 'rule of law'. It is an important part of the socialisation of children in society that they are taught the law is just, wise, good and to be obeyed. Sociologists, however, have asked, 'Who makes the law?', 'Whose interests are being protected?', and, 'Who benefits the most from laws being organised the way they are?'. Several decades of intensive research have led to the conclusion that it is the rich and powerful who benefit from the rule of law—especially as the cost of legal representation outstrips the ability of all but the most wealthy to afford it—and that most of the operation of the rule of law is directed at keeping the poor and the powerless in line. Critiquing the rule of law is not the same as advocating its overthrow, however. Rather, it is to ask questions such as, 'How could the law work better?'.

So the quest for sociological understanding involves the

sensitivity to critique. To ask the most relevant questions sociologically will include asking, 'Who benefits?' (all of society, or some much more than others?), 'Does the "golden rule" apply here?', and, 'Do those that have the gold tend to rule?'. This is the controversial character of the discipline. It is the reason why in coups d'état of both right-wing and left-wing character, sociologists have often been some of the first irritants to be disposed of by a new totalitarian regime. It is also why departments of sociology have not traditionally been found at the main establishment institutions of higher learning such as Oxford and Cambridge, or in the Australian universities such as Sydney, Melbourne or Adelaide that model themselves on the English institutions. Sociology as a discipline is taught at all these places but, unlike most other institutions throughout the world, not in separate departments of sociology but in the context of politics, education or anthropology courses.

structural and critical considerations together

Finally, some examples will illustrate how the structural and critical components of the sociological imagination operate together to provide an understanding of certain aspects of our society, especially as they relate to policies developed to deal with them. One example is the situation for endangered animal species. We face the prospect of a number of the world's animal species being hunted to extinction, or at least lost from their natural surroundings entirely, existing only in zoos. Pandas, rhinoceros and tigers are just a few on the edge of extinction. The number of tigers, for instance, is estimated to have declined by 95 per cent last century, to no more than 5000–7500 (WWF, 2000). Longer-term threats loom to many other animals, including gorillas, elephants and wolves. The dominance of homo sapiens (us) in the animal kingdom is making it difficult for others to survive. Two different processes are threatening the survival of species. The more general one is the result of the exponential growth in our world population. The clearing of rainforest, the subsistence hunting of other animals in the food chain on whom these large animals prey such as deer, pigs and wild cattle, all make survival precarious for many species.

The other more specific threat is poaching for illegal trade in body parts. There is a cultural component to this. The products, such as rhinoceros' horn or tiger parts, are valuable in Asian countries because of their supposed medicinal value. Tiger penis soup, for instance, is prescribed to restore flagging libidos! Yet even here a structural understanding is important. In a situation reminiscent of opium growers participating in the drug trade in poorer countries, so poachers faced with poverty and the need to feed families perhaps understandably see poaching as a source of economic survival. Critical thinking also helps understanding with a parallel example: the destruction of endangered species for their short-term use makes about as much sense as burning a famous bark painting to provide heating!

Another example is the official policy towards the unemployed. Some aspects of this policy are the assumptions that the cause of unemployment is lack of job skills on the part of the individual and the threat of removal of unemployment benefits after a period of time will maintain unemployed people's motivation to keep searching for jobs. Hence the requirement that training courses of some sort or another must be undertaken in order to qualify for continued benefits. Both aspects, however, are based on the assumption that the cause of unemployment exists at the individual level of the beneficiaries themselves; that the factors stopping them getting a job are to do with them personally rather than with the structural situation of the economy as a whole. Yet when the ratio of job seekers to advertised jobs goes over 30:1, the ability of individual job seekers to find employment is bound to be enormously frustrating. The requirement to take courses to retain benefits is in some ways akin to polishing up the unemployed only to put them back on the shelf at the end of the process. Let me give an example.

A young person I know was unemployed for nearly two years. As part of a new scheme, he was required to undertake a training program in order to continue to qualify for benefits. He opted for a course in training as a park ranger and thoroughly enjoyed it. As luck would have it, near the end of his course, a job vacancy was advertised for such a position. He applied keenly, only to find that he was one of more than 2000 applicants. He was devastated and is now much more cynical about his potential employability than he had been previously.

This is not to say that such training courses are not relevant. At the level of maintenance or development of self-esteem they may be important. But considering the structural level of analysis, solving the now major problem facing our societies—that there is not enough work for those who require it—will not be achieved by focusing on the individual and, in effect, blaming them for the situation in which they find themselves. Analysing the situation critically reveals a paradox: that attempts by government to wind back spending on welfare by restricting outlays in various areas have consequences in other areas. A significant proportion of the fit, active population is idle at the very time when reductions in government spending are depriving the state of the basic infrastructure of the society. Public facilities, such as schools, are poorly maintained. Walking tracks in national parks are falling into disrepair through lack of maintenance. Services providing help for the disabled and infirm are under great strain due to lack of funding. What alternative futures are possible to overcome this paradox? Some system of matching the needs in one area to the availability of solutions in another is clearly necessary.

Another example is medical negligence. Patients appear increasingly prepared to take legal action when things go wrong. Obstetrics is the most obvious example, where the payouts are substantial because they are designed to cover the financial support of a damaged infant throughout their lives. A new benchmark was set when a Sydney woman successfully sued her obstetrician for a botched delivery for $14.2 million, which was later reduced on appeal to $11 million (*The Sydney Morning Herald*, 12 August 2003). At an individual level one might argue this is highly appropriate: if doctors or other health workers provide unsatisfactory treatment then they should bear the consequences of their actions. At the structural level, however, the issues are different. In the childbirth area, some consequences are already apparent with obstetricians now acting with extreme caution, which usually means high levels of technological interventions such as caesarean section deliveries. More than that, though, the costs of malpractice insurance (professional indemnity insurance) for doctors has soared to the point where some doctors are leaving the field of practice for less risky (in a professional sense) areas or retiring altogether. According to a newspaper report the cost of indemnity insurance for obstetricians in the absence of government subsidies will be $140 000 per annum, with 45 of the nation's practicing 700 specialist obstetricians leaving practice in 2001 alone (*The Sydney Morning Herald*, 12 August 2003). For general practitioners who practise obstetrics it has become a risk to their livelihoods, which many can do without. More than one-third of general practitioner–obstetricians in Australia stopped delivering babies in the five-year period 1988–93

(*The Age*, 18 November 1993), with particular consequences for rural areas. Another 40% drop was reported for the five-year period 1996–2001 (AWA, 2001). If this trend continues, it may become difficult to find an obstetrician willing to handle particularly complicated deliveries, as is now the case in a number of large American cities, particularly New York.

Using a critical sensibility, clearly, incompetent doctors should not be able to continue to practice if they are a danger to the public. But equally clear is that the eventual consequences of increasing litigiousness are also undesirable. Attention needs to be given in a social policy sense (of alternative futures) to maximising the individual competence of doctors without diminishing the availability of competent medical services at the structural level.

The final example of how the structural and critical sensitivities operate together is the phenomenon of the mass killings that have shocked both Australians and New Zealanders in recent times. The examples at home are becoming legion: Hoddle Street and Queen Street in Melbourne, Strathfield in Sydney, Hillcrest and Hanging Rock in Queensland, Port Arthur in Tasmania, as well as at Aramoana near Dunedin in New Zealand. Multiple victim shootings by a lone gunman have caused great anguish in societies accustomed to only reading about these events taking place in the United States. My mind is concentrated on these events as I regularly commute past the spot on Hoddle Street in Melbourne (and did so a few hours earlier on the fateful day itself) where a grove of eucalypts now stands as a memorial to the slain.

The individual level of understanding is obviously very important to analysing these events. The individuals concerned and their states of psychological health are very relevant. But the individual level of analysis is not enough; an understanding of the structural level is also needed. Here it is necessary to consider such aspects as a culture of masculinity in which both violence towards others is an acceptable solution to personal difficulties (reflected in such phenomena as domestic violence), and guns are akin to an expression of masculinity itself. Attempts to restrict the availability of weapons, in particular automatic guns for which there can be no reasonable justification for allowing public ownership in peacetime, have met with staunch opposition from vocal lobby groups. Observe groups of small boys (not girls) playing together. Playing with toy guns and simulating shootings are very much a part of the socialisation into masculine culture that young boys undergo. Parents who refuse to allow their children to have toy guns find their sons turning any stick or Lego® construction into a weapon shape. Then there are other structural considerations, including how we are desensitised to violence by the continual exposure to mainly American television and movie scripts in which gratuitous violence, filled with Rambo-like cult figures, is part of virtually every plot. Video games also glorify violence—one such game was advertised, complete with marketing language, 'You'll soon be up to your waist in blood and guts!'.

We also need to consider the situation in which these unfortunate individuals find themselves. As all the inquests into the various shootings have found, there are many individuals like these gunmen in the community. In the context of the running down of public mental health services, deinstitutionalisation of the mentally ill and the possible isolation of individuals even in small communities, it is virtually certain such calamities will occur again.

Again, it is worth explaining since this is an aspect of the sociological imagination that is sometimes misunderstood, which is not to say that the individuals concerned are not responsible for their actions and should not face the consequences. What I am saying is that focusing on the individual alone leaves an explanation incomplete. In a sense, the perpetrators are victims themselves. Furthermore, we will not get very far in our attempts to understand social phenomena like these slayings, to be able to prevent them occurring in the future, unless we consider the wider context in which they take place. Likewise with the availability of guns. While they greatly exacerbate the dangers of violence, from a structural perspective, no one suggests that restricting gun usage to law enforcement officers would somehow 'solve' the social problems faced in our society. Although guns make the violence much worse, the underlying causes of violence are not guns per se, but other more social factors, including poverty and racism.

conclusion

This chapter has considered the structural and critical aspects of the sociological imagination. I have argued here and in the previous chapter that the quest for a sociological understanding of a particular phenomenon involves exercising the four sensibilities, which are historical, cultural, structural and critical. Engaging in sociological analysis of some aspect of the social world requires a consideration of each of these aspects in turn. Each is partial, but together they represent the hallmark of a sociological way of understanding the social world.

6 the social and the biological world

Having outlined the four sensibilities involved in developing an adequate sociological analysis, I propose now to illustrate one important way in which they can be used: to analyse and discuss the boundary between the natural and the social worlds. The debate about the relative importance of environment and hereditary factors, about nature and nurture, is a long one and has all sorts of political implications. To what extent is biology social destiny? To what extent is the way a person turns out as he or she grows from childhood to adulthood the result of the particular genetic configuration they received at birth, and to what extent is it the result of the social experiences they have while growing up? The answers are complex and difficult to do justice to in a book of this size and introductory character. But they clearly involve some combination of both factors; the debate is where the relative emphasis should be put.

the social and biological worlds

The nature–nurture debate has intensified in recent years with the advent of the Human Genome Project, the huge scientific project based in the United States in which molecular biologists and geneticists mapped the human genetic structure. The potential for genetic engineering is that much closer. Certain diseases which have historically caused enormous suffering may eventually be eliminated. But some aspects of the program are controversial, especially in the area of behavioural genetics. Critics of the project, however, say it puts too much emphasis on genetic causes of behaviour and too little on environmental and social causes (see Hubbard and Wald, 1993).

How does a sociological imagination inform these debates? How do sociologists differentiate between the social and the biological world? Sociologists, while accepting the importance of genetic/hereditary factors, have generally tended to stress more the environment/nurture side of the continuum. In other words, they would generally stress the importance of the social in drawing the boundary between the social and the biological world.

The need to differentiate the effects of the natural as against the social world is well established amongst sociologists. This is reflected in the conceptual terminology used and a couple of important conceptual distinctions can be made. The first concerns how the period in the life course of an individual from the age of about twelve to 25 years should be conceptualised. Should it be seen as the period of *adolescence* or of *youth*? 'Adolescence' is the term most often used in medical and other circles to refer to a particular stage of physical and psychological development in the human life cycle culminating in 'maturity'. In sociological terms, however, this concept is not very useful for analysing the complex social and cultural factors affecting young people's lives, when they are no longer children but are not yet accepted as adults. (The concept of adolescence is of relatively recent historical origin and refers to young people in industrialised countries.)

Historically, the transition between childhood and adulthood for all but the children of the affluent was much shorter and harsher. However, in industrialised countries at least, the abolition of child labour, the extension of the period of full-time education and the continuing economic dependence on parents, often well into a person's third decade of life, has created a time characterised by ambiguity which is most usefully described as 'youth'. In today's times of casualised and generally poor job opportunities, as well as declining housing affordability, it is perhaps much harder for a greater proportion of young people to move out of home and establish their own independent livelihood and living arrangements than it was for their parents a generation ago. 'Adult children' in their twenties living at home with their parents are a common occurrence today. The key features of this period in a person's life cannot be tightly defined as a biophysiological category. When it begins and ends has enormous variation. Indeed, there is nothing biologically determined about the experience of young people; their experience is the outcome of changing historical, cultural and structural circumstances. Does the 21st birthday party today retain the element of marking the status passage from child to adult as it may have done in the past? Does anyone actually get their first key to the family home at 21?

Another essential distinction is between *sex* and *gender*. Sex refers to the biological differences between men and women, especially in genitalia. Gender refers to the meaning attached to being male or female, both historically and culturally. Little girls traditionally wear pink clothing while little boys wear blue. These are the colours we have come to associate with being male or female. At this time, both historically and culturally, these are the social meanings that have become attached to the fact of being male or female. As with ethnicity it is important to note that everyone has a gender; it is not something that only women have, which is how it is sometimes used!

The distinction between sex and gender is necessary because the biological does not determine the social; biology is of minimal importance with regard to the place of women (or men) in any society. The range of meaning attached to being female or male in any society varies enormously, culturally and historically. The social construction of the meaning of being male or female is usually discussed in terms of the concepts of *masculinity* and *femininity*. Sociologists have found it useful to talk about masculinity and femininity as social practices; that is, as being grounded in practical actions in terms of what people do. In this way they are able to talk about gendered practices, such as wearing pink or blue, as social not biological.

An example of gender difference is the attitude towards body hair. For many Western women in this historical period, body hair in armpits, on legs and on 'bikini lines' is something to be removed, often with considerable discomfort. This is not something that men in our society usually worry about, except on their faces. One sometimes hears the argument that it is more 'natural' for women to remove body hair. Our bulsh detector should switch to 'red alert' here. It is, of course, nothing of the sort, but a part of the traditional social practice of femininity, acknowledging that there are *social mores* (behavioural expectations) in this historical and cultural context for women to shave their legs. Once again, a wander through an art gallery will show you how recent this concern this. Luxurious tufts of armpit hair on the female as well as the male figures were common. Our sociological imagination should make us extremely sceptical whenever claims about something being more natural are made.

The development of a particular sociological language or jargon can also be seen as an attempt to be precise about issues such as the boundary between the social and the biological worlds. Three examples will make this clearer. First, it is easy to show, using a cultural sensibility, that certain supposed biological categories are in fact culturally based. In an earlier example we saw how the condition of 'wind' or colic in babies is culturally dealt with; it exists as a biological disease category in one society but not in another. The meaning of a baby's wind depends on the society you are in. In the United Kingdom, wind in babies existed while in (the then) Czechoslovakia, it didn't. Or more to the point, in one country it was considered a problem that had to be dealt with, while in the other it was considered an unproblematic aspect of the feeding of babies.

The second example to be explored concerns the ratio of women to men and what has been called the 'missing 77 million women' (Sen, 1992). On the terrain of sex—that is, from the science of human reproductive biology—we know that about five per cent more boys than girls are born. But women are biologically hardier than men and, if both sexes receive the same care, women survive better than men at all ages (Waldron, 1983). So the sex ratio that would be expected is about 105 women to every 100 men. But the gender ratio, which is a different measure reflecting the outcome of social conditions, can be different.

In most Western countries, such as the United States, Canada, Australia, New Zealand, Great Britain and France, the sex ratio and the gender ratio coincide. Women outnumber men. The ratio is roughly 105 women for every 100 men. In many countries of Asia and North Africa, however, the pattern is very different. The sex ratio (that is, from reproductive biology) continues at 105:100 but the gender ratio does not. In Egypt the ratio is 95 females for every 100 males; in Bangladesh, China and West Africa, 94:100; in India, 93:100; and in Pakistan, 90:100. The difference between the sex ratio that should be expected and the gender ratio of what actually occurs is estimated by the United Nations to amount to 77 million women. There are vastly fewer women than reproductive biology would lead us to expect. Why?

The quest for a sociological explanation for these startling figures begins by asking, 'What is it about the way those societies are organised that might explain the difference?'. The answer needs historical, cultural, structural and critical sensibilities. If the proportion of women to men is substantially less than would be expected and less than other countries in the world, there must be aspects of the way those societies are organised that will account for the difference. Sen (1992) points to a range of practices that help explain these figures, all resulting from the organisation of the societies in question, which systematically favour men over women—this is, what is meant when discussing patriarchal societies. The documented practices include abortion of female foetuses (after mothers are advised they are carrying girls), and female infanticide (smothering or poisoning at birth). There is also the systematic and selective favouring of boys with regard to food, education and healthcare (if there's not enough to go around, it's the boys who get whatever there is), which results in higher mortality rates for girls (see Koenig and D'Sousa, 1986). It could also be that girls are not considered sufficiently important to count in official figures or that births of girl babies are hidden where there is compulsory restriction of family size. All these result from the relative powerlessness of women in relation to men; an issue important in explaining why HIV/AIDS is a heterosexual pandemic in Africa, as we saw earlier. In other words, the gender ratio is a social phenomenon. The quest for sociological explanation involves invoking a historical, cultural and structural sensibility to explore how it results from the social organisation of the societies in question.

'How could it be otherwise?' This is the classic question asked as part of a critical sensibility. What alternative futures are there for young women growing up in these countries? How can the relative neglect of females in these societies be overcome? An exception to the pattern outlined above is the key to answering that question. The Indian state of Kerala is one of the poorest on the subcontinent, yet it has a female to male gender ratio of 104:100. Kerala also has the most developed school system in India (over 90 per cent of the population are literate), as well as a highly developed and extensive healthcare system. For the Nairs, one of the major ethnic groups that comprise Kerala society, property inheritance passes through the female line (Sen, 1992: 587). The consequence of this is that the gender ratio more closely approximates the sex ratio.

The third example is that of Kenyan athletes. Why have Kenyan male athletes dominated middle- and long-distance running at Olympic Games? What combination of social and biological factors result in such success? In my local sports store there is a series of huge posters advertising a brand of sporting footwear with the theme, 'In my mind I am a Kenyan'. And Kenyans have been successful; since the 1960 Olympic Games in Rome, in the middle- and long-distance track races for men (800 metres to 10 000 metres), athletes from this small African country (nowadays sometimes running for other countries) have won 47 medals. The next highest tally is sixteen won by athletes from Great Britain, followed by Ethiopia with fifteen, New Zealand and Morocco with nine (DatabaseOlympics.com, 2010). How has this country of only 29 million people, one of the poorest countries in the world with a Gross National Product per head of about

$350 in 1998 (World Bank, 2000), managed to produce so many fine athletes? What is the relative importance of nature and nurture in explaining one of the major features of world track competition in recent decades?

Some biological factors, such as race, may be partially responsible. African and African-American athletes dominate world track and field in general, and in particular African-American athletes dominate the sprinting events. In the 2008 Beijing Olympics only two of a possible 30 medals were won by athletes of Caucasian racial background in all men's track events up to the marathon, excluding the relays. It appears white men can't run (or jump!) though there are likely to be cultural factors at work here too.

A second factor in the terrain of biology is the well-known physiological effects of training at altitude. With a sizeable portion of Kenya more than 1000 metres above sea level, the beneficial effects of growing up and training at higher altitudes are reflected in enhanced performances at sea level. Yet these aspects of explanation are only partial. Why would the biological advantage be bestowed on Kenyan athletes, and why not on the athletes of surrounding countries, such as Tanzania, Zaire or Nigeria? Many other countries have high altitude areas but have not produced world-class athletes; for example, Nepal. Most importantly, though, if these biophysiological factors are so important, why do they only benefit men? Do Kenyan women somehow miss out on the advantage for running fast? The first medal (a silver) ever to be won by a Kenyan woman track-and-field athlete occurred only at the Atlanta Olympics in 1996. Only at the Beijing Olympics in 2008 did Kenyan women begin to emulate their illustrious male counterparts with three medals including two golds. It is therefore necessary to consider the social world to begin a sociological quest for explanation.

The four sociological sensibilities are important here. *Historically*, Kenya has links through colonialism with Great Britain and a British tradition of athletics was imported into the schooling system from the early days. A similar argument would hold for the relative success of New Zealand in these events. This formed a culture in which athletics, rather than basketball or baseball, was a favoured sporting activity. *Culturally*, there is the importance of role models and imitation. When the sporting heroes of the country are athletes, all kids want to emulate them and win at those races; the races in which the sporting heroes excel on the international stage are the most prestigious ones (such as the sprints or middle-distance events). A part of the socialisation of young males appears to be idolisation of national sporting heroes. A parallel Australian example is cricket. When fast bowlers Dennis Lillee and Jeff Thomson were the pin-up boys of Australian cricket in the early 1980s, kids everywhere wanted to be fast bowlers and you would see them marking out huge run-ups halfway to the boundary and tearing in. In more recent times, Shane Warne became the cricket hero—many kids then wanted to be a spin bowler and the run-ups shortened dramatically! Lots of young boys want to be like AFL (Australian Football League) footballer Gary Ablett Jr, League player Greg Inglis or All Black rugby star Dan Carter. Thus it is easy to see how a talented young Kenyan sportsman might decide to concentrate on middle-distance running rather than some other distance or some other sport. Similarly you would expect a talented young African-American or African-Canadian to concentrate on sprinting events. Imitation of those sports and events in which their country has a major world presence is only to be expected.

Structural factors to do with the organisation of society are also relevant. Being a poor country, with a poorly developed transport infrastructure, including few school buses, it is common for young Kenyans to walk and run long distances to and from school, in effect training from an early age. Then there is considerable money to be made from athletics, especially from road races in affluent countries. Success in the international arena is a means of social mobility in monetary terms as well as status, with national and international recognition.

In addition, like many societies, preference may be given to boys rather than girls in the encouragement to pursue sporting activities; a result of a society structured in such a way that an unequal share of resources is accorded to men over women, in the manner argued in the example of the 'missing' women above. The behavioural expectations for young women, what are termed the 'social mores', mean that Kenyan women of child-bearing age have traditionally been expected to drop out of running and have children.

A *critical* sensibility asks, 'How could it be otherwise?'. For instance, how might Kenyan women be able to take advantage of the favourable environment towards athletics so as to emulate their male counterparts? Some of this is already occurring with several world-ranked Kenyan juniors among women athletes and more Olympic medals as mentioned. Note the emphasis here is not only on how young Kenyan women might be encouraged to pursue athletics—in other words, by better individual adjustment to existing social and cultural conditions—but also how Kenyan society might facilitate greater participation of women athletes. All these sociological issues would need to be taken into account to complement the biologically based ones in order to develop an adequate explanation for this remarkable sporting achievement.

The boundary between the social world and the natural world is not rigidly drawn: the sociological quest involves carefully investigating where the boundary lies. A critical sensibility involves asking, '*How do you know?*' and our sociological bulsh detector is in regular use. In particular, it involves an awareness or sensitivity to explanations for social phenomena being made on biological grounds ('but it's only natural'). The implications of such an explanation is that this is the only possible order of things; that being based on biology or genetics, the existing social order is somehow fixed, immutable and unchangeable. Asking, '*How could it be otherwise?*', involves a sensitivity to the possibilities for change and to alternative futures.

Investigating the boundary between biology and culture is also important when the issues appear to be mainly social. Let's consider as an example a major social policy decision being faced in the Australian context: 'What would be an appropriate size for the population of this country by the middle of next century?'. How many more people than the current 22 million would be an appropriate level? Should it be a minimal increase to perhaps 25 million by the year 2050, or would 30 million or maybe 50 million be an appropriate target? All of these have been suggested in recent debates as the question of migration levels has become highly politicised.

The social policy question has been cast primarily in social terms because the rate of natural increase (from births) is likely to make a minimal impact on future population growth. Instead, the level of immigration from other countries is likely to determine the population level. What should the migrant intake be? Given the large numbers of actual and potential trouble spots in the world, the misery of displaced people from around the world portrayed nightly on our television screens, the huge numbers of refugees seeking new homes, let alone vast numbers in other poorer countries who might choose to migrate to countries such as

Australia should the opportunity arise, what policies should be pursued by governments?

The planning question clearly hinges in a considerable way on the implications of another three, eight or 33 million people. What would be the implications even of the modest increase to say 25 million by the year 2050? Given the clearly expressed historical preference for Australians, recently arrived or otherwise, to live 'between the desert and the beach', and in particular in urban areas near the coastline, what would be the implications of another two or three cities the size of Sydney or Melbourne? Would the additional population provide larger domestic markets, and therefore be likely to enhance the standard of living and quality of life for all Australians as some economists claim? Or, given the current difficulty of providing employment for all those who require it, would these problems be compounded by another eight million people? What would be the implications for some notion of social cohesion for Australia as a nation of such a population increase? Would one likely implication be the decline of the urban core as has occurred in the United States, another major country in the world built upon immigration? Would the implication be that some Australian cities may become like some of the most dangerous American cities, such as Washington, Los Angeles and New York?

The social side of the question is also not the whole story. Environmental considerations involve not only social aspects but also those concerned with water, air quality and so on, which are also likely to influence decisions about the ability to sustain population increases on what is, after all, the driest continent as climate change in the direction of global warming tightens its grip. Although countries such as Australia have a low density of population by world standards, much of the continent is unsuitable or only marginally suitable for settlement. More than 200 years of white settlement of the continent has shown that clearly. The toll on the environment, on water, air and forests, of even another three million, let alone another eight or 33 million, is likely to be significant. Already attempts to increase agricultural production have resulted in significant environmental degradation in the form of rising salination, deforestation, the fouling and destruction of waterways and the like. So social planning questions about Australia's future will increasingly take these issues into account. As Furze (2008) argues, environmental problems are at their base social problems. So environmental considerations combining both the social and biological will determine the outcome of the question of alternative futures in population size at the level of political process.

The boundary between the biological and the social world, between nature and culture, is not easy to specify. Recent developments in sociology are concerned with *deconstructing* the divide; that is, showing how the relationship is a complex one in which the categories themselves (such as nature/culture or sex/gender) are not easily defined or separated (see Turner, 1992).

biological determinism and ideology

The debate about the relative importance of the social and the biological has broader dimensions that require the exercising of the sociological sensibilities. In human history, the idea that biology is destiny has been a very powerful one. It is called *biological determinism* because it involves the idea that your biology at birth (black/white, male/female) will decide your chances in life. In other words, it accords a primary role for *ascribed status* (the personal characteristics you are born with) rather than *achieved status* (what you make of your life). It is an ideology in the sense that it is a set of ideas that justify a course of action.

This ideology of biological determinism has been called 'Social Darwinism'. It took Darwin's basic idea about the 'survival of the fittest' and applied it to human societies (see Rose et al., 1984). According to this ideology, those who were 'fittest' were obviously those who had 'done best' by the contemporary criteria for assessing success in a society. Those who did not 'make it' were obviously less well equipped on the terrain of biology to 'succeed'. This ideology has been a powerful one, serving to *legitimate* (make seem right and proper) existing power structures and inequality, especially those based upon racism and sexism (see Gould, 1981). Unequal opportunities for men and women that exist are often 'explained' in terms of female biology. In tennis, for example, the difference in the prize money at stake between the men's and women's finals in many of the world's leading tennis tournaments is 'explained' in terms of the frailness of women in playing only best-of-three instead of best-of-five sets. In other words, the social is reduced to the biological to make aspects of inequalities seem 'natural' and therefore inevitable. Only in 2007 did the organisers of the last of the four major tennis 'Grand Slam' events, Wimbledon, after considerable social pressure, pay equal prize money to the winners of the men's and women's singles (Altius Directory, 2010).

In today's society, the ideology of biological determination underlies theories and debates such as those suggesting a link between race and measures of intelligence. Invoking biological determinism legitimates exclusion policies. These policies include cuts in taxes that attempt to ameliorate the effects of a market economy to maintain social cohesion, the abolition of social welfare programs, the jettisoning of various affirmative-action employment programs, as well as the tightening of immigration requirements. Social control, not social amelioration, becomes the primary objective.

On the other hand, progressive social policies have attempted to challenge some of the effects of the ideology of biological determinism; to seek to make achieved status rather than ascribed status the basis for the distribution of social rewards in society as a means of trying to maximise human potential. Inclusive social policies have attempted to bring groups who may be marginal into the mainstream of society. The abolition of apartheid in South Africa was an important move in this direction. Black South Africans are now able to live, marry and seek the jobs they want, while these choices were previously barred to them on the basis of the ascribed characteristic of race.

Historically, however, the trend throughout much of the world, including Western countries, is towards inequalities being magnified and entrenched with considerable implications for the social cohesion and political stability of a society. One effect is with the political process where large swings in voter preferences, especially towards ultra-conservative parties, have been a feature of the political landscape. In the context of structural change to the economies of societies through globalisation, the 'politics of blame' have led to an unfortunate process of scapegoating on racial grounds (Indigenous people, Asian migrants), a form of biological determinism.

conclusion

The quest for sociological understanding involves attention to the four features of explanation outlined in this book. One of the important ways in which such a sociological imagination can be used is to push back the conventionally held notions of the boundary between the natural and the social world. It is an ongoing debate, with new developments occurring all the time. For example, exciting possibilities are on the horizon, such as the elimination of some genetic diseases. A sociological imagination, however, is important to balance this debate. Our sociological bulsh detector remains important, particularly when explanations about the biological terrain for social phenomena begin to be used as a rationale for social and political programs that accept the status quo as inevitable or somehow 'natural', and therefore immutable. The sense of critique and the search for alternative futures remain central to the sociological quest.

7 theory and method

Having a historical, cultural, structural and critical sensibility is crucial to the sociological quest. Now we can consider exactly how the insights generated by those sensibilities can be used in social analysis. This will be addressed by introducing the idea of sociological theories or perspectives, each with their own way of conceptualising the relationships. The links between theory and research will also be considered; that is, how we actually *do* sociology.

doing sociology

Students who come to sociology are often dismayed by the apparent lack of agreement between sociologists on how the sociological quest should proceed and, at times, even what constitutes the discipline. Not all sociologists would agree with the introduction to the discipline this book represents. Some writers find it more appropriate to talk about 'sociologies' than sociology (for example, Austin, 1984). This is sometimes called the 'untidy face' of sociology and is another way of saying there is no single body of knowledge, theories or methods common to all sociologists. Actually, the lack of theoretical agreement is a sign of a living, evolving discipline which thrives on lively debates, not only over different theories but also over different methods, conflicting findings and the quality of evidence. The caricature that I have heard is that 'you ask two sociologists for their view on something and you get ten different opinions!' What there is, is a collection of different ways of thinking that are variously called perspectives, approaches, theories, schools of thought or traditions.

The perspective or theoretical approach affects the conduct of research when we come to make sociological explanations. For many, if not most, sociologists the hallmark of a sociological way of approaching social phenomena is the concern with the integration of theory and method; integration in the sense of each being moulded and shaped by the other. The theoretical approach taken determines to a considerable extent the conduct of subsequent social research since the different perspectives generate certain sorts of research problems, which in turn favour certain sorts of methods for doing research.

What is a theory? *Theory* is a central element of all academic disciplines and all sciences. A theory is a statement that explains the nature of a relationship between concepts or ideas. Earlier we considered a theory about the relationship between external threat and internal solidarity in a society. Theory is necessary to begin to make sense of the 'facts'; that is, to interpret and give them meaning. Sometimes a distinction is drawn between theory, which is assumed to be somehow the 'ivory tower', and practice, which is more concrete and more useful. Behind every practical course of action, however, lies a theoretical basis for it. Often, spelling out the theory involves detailing the implicit bases or principles that make 'the facts' intelligible. Both theory and practice are closely related and both are important to the sociological quest.

In the early chapters, sociology was defined as a social science involving a quest for explanations based on a rational appeal to impartial evidence. This chapter considers the nature of different sorts of explanations and the issue of evidence and how we 'know' things about the social world. The term used for this questioning of how we know things is 'epistemology'. An example of an epistemological question is if I am asked how I know what the meaning is of someone, say, gesturing towards someone else with two fingers held upwards! This is to recall the infamous incident on a trip to Australia when the then president of the United States, on departing from an official function, gave what he assumed was a victory sign to his hosts! Considering these questions will demonstrate how the foundations of sociology lie within philosophy, and the differences between the major sociological perspectives have their origins within the discipline of philosophy.

Method is used here to refer to the process of collecting information or data about the social world. The commonplace conception of the primary sociological method is the question-naire—a series of written questions asked of the respondent by the interviewer, either in person or by mail, phone, email or on the internet. But there are many other ways of answering the question, 'How do you know?'. We 'know' about the social world by conducting empirical research on some aspect or aspects of it. Asking some questions rather than others will affect the sort of information collected and the sorts of findings likely to be made. Theory, method and findings or results shape and mould each other. The important point is that information or data about the social world does not exist in some free-floating, independent way. Instead, it exists as the answer to a sociological question or problem which makes its gathering and interpretation relevant. Another way of saying this is that a concern with the unity of theory and method is central to the quest for sociological understanding.

This concern with the unity of theory and method is often used to differentiate sociology from journalism, the latter usually being concerned with more immediate aspects of social issues and not with the underlying theoretical aspects of the process of knowing about the social world. Different theories have different means of approaching social phenomena, but their unifying feature, and indeed the feature which gives the discipline its defining characteristic and coherence, is the issue of the place of the individual in the larger scheme of things. How is it that despite our individuality, our unique experiences and our differences, we all manage to behave socially and be part of a collective entity known as a society?

In discussing the main perspectives of the discipline, there are some aspects to bear in mind. First, there is no fixed, uniformly agreed upon idea of what the major perspectives are. They are called different names by different sociologists, and there is disagreement on the extent to which the different perspectives overlap. What is presented below in more detail as the three main perspectives of classical sociology—functionalism, conflict theory and interactionism—would be agreed upon by probably most, but by no means all, sociologists. Within each there is a variety of different approaches and differences between the approaches, which result from different historical, geographical and social circumstances. What is presented here is an attempt to classify these approaches, to illustrate them. As you delve further into the study of the discipline of sociology, you will be introduced to more contemporary perspectives that critique some or all of these classical perspectives. Some of these contemporary perspectives for studying society include postmodernism, poststructuralism, feminist theory and cultural studies. For now, however, I have taken the approach of introducing a fairly conventional understanding of the sociological imagination, as a building block upon which, and against which, other theoretical approaches can be developed in any further studies the reader may take in sociology.

Second, while all sociologists work to a greater or lesser extent within certain perspectives, they do not go around wearing badges identifying what their preferred perspective is. To some extent, at least, it is possible to draw on more than one perspective in seeking to understand and analyse a particular sociological problem.

Third, having a perspective is unavoidable. In order to focus our attention to even begin to make sense of something, we need some selectivity. So there is no such thing as a perspectiveless sociological account. There are only differing degrees of implicitness and explicitness of that perspective. This point applies to all academic disciplines, including the natural and physical sciences, not just to sociology.

In some sciences though, the perspective or *paradigm*, as it is sometimes called, is accepted to the point where it is taken for granted. Astronomy, for instance, operates with a heliocentric perspective of the universe. The sun is at the centre of the solar system and the planets revolve around it. Yet until Copernicus showed this to be the case in the sixteenth century, astronomy was based on the geocentric paradigm proposed by Ptolemy, where the Earth was held to be at the centre of the universe. Likewise in medicine: the late-nineteenth and early-twentieth century is marked by the gradual rise to dominance of the so-called germ theory of disease. Different perspectives or theories of disease are followed by the modalities of so-called alternative medicine, such as chiropractic, naturopathy and homoeopathy. All these are theories of the causation of ill health in the sense that they are statements about the relationship between health and other factors.

So what are these sociological perspectives? At their most elementary, they are simply a point of view. More than that, however, they may be defined as a relatively coherent tradition of ideas about the world and how it works. In sociology they tend to go by the name either of the major person who was responsible for giving coherence to the perspective as we know it today, or of the major idea they encompass. While they all propose a way of studying the relationship between the individual and society, they differ in two main ways. First, they make mutually incompatible philosophical assumptions about the objects of study, the nature of the individual and of society, and the relationship between the two. Second, they disagree about the meaning and validity of the knowledge derived from the particular perspectives; that is, on the status of the knowledge derived from the particular perspectives. I will deal with this point later in the chapter to stress the link between the perspective taken and the method adopted for studying the social world.

the underlying assumptions

One of the bases on which the perspectives can be differentiated is by the positions they take on the major philosophical debates which underlie the social sciences. (My aim here is to introduce the sociological representations of some major philosophical issues and debates.) These positions take the form of assumptions in the sense of not being empirically testable but existing at the philosophical level. These assumptions tend to be dualistic; that is, the debates are presented as contrasting pairs with each perspective taking a position in relation to one side or the other. Mostly they can be represented as a continuum in which one takes a position at one end or the other. It should be remembered that my treatment of these issues only scratches the surface of the substantial debates in the philosophy of the social sciences, but it gives some basis for understanding how the major perspectives of sociology differ from other disciplines.

The first set of these assumptions concerns the *nature of the individual*. This is basically a set of assumptions about human nature. Is human nature more self-centred or altruistic, more competitive or cooperative, more rational or irrational? These are basically untestable propositions about which one makes assumptions. To put it another way, the question, 'What is human nature?', is not empirically resolvable. The two basic philosophical positions are Thomas Hobbes' (philosopher, 1588–1679) pessimistic view of human nature and the more optimistic position espoused by Jean Jacques Rousseau (philosopher, 1712–78). When Anne Frank wrote in her diary near the end of her time in hiding from the Nazis in wartime Amsterdam, and near the subsequent end of her life in a concentration camp, 'In spite of everything, I still believe people are really good at heart', she was taking a clear Rousseauean position. If she had, perhaps understandably, come to the view of the inherent evilness of the occupying Nazis, she would have been taking a more Hobbesian position.

The *nature of society* is the second set of assumptions. One debate here is whether society exists only in human consciousness (the subjectivist position), or whether it has an independent existence (the objectivist position). The terms 'objective' and 'subjective' are not used here in their commonsense meanings, concerning whether one's values are involved or not. Rather, this huge philosophical debate revolves around the question of the nature of reality. One nice example to illustrate this debate is how it has come to light that up-market clothing stores, in a marketing strategy aimed at flattery to improve sales, are resizing women's clothes. Clothes that had carried a size twelve label are now being labelled size ten, what many regard (historically and culturally) as the ideal body size. Size fourteen clothes are likewise being relabelled size twelve, and so on. One chain in particular, selling clothes under the Country Road label, has applied for the change to be recognised officially by the relevant government standards authority that defines the sizes; that is, what configuration of hip, waist and bust measurements objectively constitutes which size. The authority has indicated there will be no change in official sizing measurements. Its position is an objectivist one, there is an objective reality in which certain measurements 'mean' size ten. The clothing chain, by contrast, is operating with a subjectivist position on clothing sizes, socially constructing the meaning of size ten in the hope that sales will be improved by more women fitting clothes with a label indicating small-sized clothes.

In other countries the sizing of clothes is even more confusing. In the United States, for instance, while men's clothing sizes tend to be standard (a certain combination of waist, chest and neck size 'objectively means' a particular clothing size), for women the situation is more complex. There exists no industry-wide sizing standards in the US$130 billion annual apparel market. There appears to be no similar uniform objectivist measurements of what combination of hip, waist and bust measurement means what size. The result is that buying clothes is much more complex (and organised on a subjectivist basis) because you might require a particular size of clothing in one shop and another size elsewhere. Indeed, it has been reported that the mail-order outlet of one large manufacturer of women's clothes uses different sizing measurements from its own retail outlets (*The Wall Street Journal*, 11 November 1994).

Arguing a subjectivist position on the nature of society would indicate that people construct in their minds an entity called 'Australian society' or 'New Zealand society', helped along by symbols which represent the entity, such as flags, national anthems, silver ferns and wallabies, or particular colour combinations, be they green and gold or black and white. Related to this is the debate about whether society is more than the sum of its individual parts or just the sum of the individuals who comprise it. Already the reader may be able to see some of the positions I have taken so far in this book. Earlier I made the argument that society is more than the sum of its parts. This is in the same way that a cake cannot be considered to be just the sum of its ingredients—the act of cooking (or by analogy, living in society) modifies some of the individualistic elements.

A third assumption is the *nature of social change*, about whether change in society occurs because of an evolutionary or revolutionary basis. Evolutionary social change is gradual, incremental and small-scale. Revolutionary social change, by contrast, is more large-scale. Should the major changes occurring in Australian and New Zealand society associated with globalisation and the restructuring of their economies in the name of the ideologies of 'compete or perish' and 'level playing fields' be considered evolutionary or revolutionary social change? Should the events that have occurred in South Africa, the Middle East or Indonesia be considered evolutionary or revolutionary?

Likewise, should we regard smaller-scale changes in the way our society operates as evolutionary or revolutionary? Think of changes in the social acceptability of smoking, particularly in public places. Or perhaps the variable extent of changes among Caucasians in culturally valued body colouring—from tanned to what has been called a 'peaches and cream' complexion— associated with concerns about skin cancer and holes in the ozone layer. Do these changes follow from earlier changes or are they of a markedly different nature?

Another related set of assumptions concerns *the relation-ship between the individual and society*. First among these is the debate over the basis for the social order. How does the society in which we live manage to exist and survive over time? One answer is on the basis of consensus: we basically have shared values and agree on what is necessary for social order to continue. The sanctity of human life and property is one of these shared values. The other position is that social order is only possible on the basis of coercion. Conflict occurs between groups in society with different values, in which more powerful social groups impose their will over and control less powerful groups. This is the basis of social order. The sanctity of human life and property is maintained by a large and active police presence. Those who benefit most from the value of the sanctity of property are those who have most of it.

The second assumption made about the relationship between the individual and society arises out of the major philosophical debate about the extent of *determinism and free will* in the conduct of human affairs. There are various types of determinism; here I am only concerned with the question in a broad context. To what extent do the expectations of others and of the society as a whole determine our individual actions, or do we have free will to decide for ourselves? A major decision commonly faced by young people in establishing an adult identity is whether they will formalise their principal emotional and sexual relationship by actually getting married. Will they respond to the frequent expectations of others, such as parents, by actually 'tying the knot'? To take a position at one end of this continuum is to argue we are determined to a greater or lesser extent by the expectations others have of us. To take a position at the other end of the continuum is to argue we have free will to choose to respond to those expectations or to ignore them.

A French school of philosophy known as existentialism, whose principal figure was Jean-Paul Sartre, takes the position at the pole of the continuum. Individuals always have choice and free will to decide their actions. So you can never say as a way of being released from responsibility for your actions that you had no choice. You are acting in 'bad faith' (that is, deceiving yourself) if you do. Lest you think of this as an esoteric debate with little relevance, it was the basis for the Nuremberg trials, one of the most important legal events of last century. The basis on which the Nazi defendants were prosecuted as war criminals and on which a number of them were executed was the disallowing of what has come to be called the Eichmann defence: they were just following orders. The case against them was based on the argument that they had free will. Indeed, if enough had refused to follow orders the war crimes would not have occurred.

A sociological representation of this philosophical debate is the distinction outlined in a previous chapter between agency and structure. The question revolves around whether people produce society or are determined by it; the role of individual human agency as against the constraints and determinants of action arising from the expectations of others. This theme is explored extensively in the classic introduction to the discipline by Peter Berger (1963).

The other major philosophical debate for our purposes here is that which requires assumptions to be made between *materialism and idealism*. The use of these terms has nothing to do with their commonsense association with one being materialistic or idealistic. Rather, the debate refers to what has priority, what comes first: people's material existence or their ideas. The famous quote from Karl Marx that social being determines consciousness epitomises the materialist position. For Marx, the position you hold in society (expressed as your class position) will determine your ideas about the world. From an idealist position, the reverse is argued; the ideas people hold will affect their social location.

So it is possible to have materialist and idealist strategies of social change. For Marx this involved the extreme lengths of changing the economic basis on which society operated. Idealist solutions rely more on educating people differently, that is, changing their ideas.

the three major perspectives

Having considered very briefly the main underlying philosophical debates that together provide one basis for differentiating between theoretical perspectives, the three major traditional perspectives of sociology, in terms of the positions they take on these debates about the individual and society, will now be outlined. These perspectives are commonly known as *functionalism*, *conflict theory* and *interactionism*. Outlined here is one quite common characterisation of the complexity of perspectives. Many other perspectives exist, but most are variations to a greater or lesser extent on these major three. Only the major points will be outlined here; all have been subjected to much critical examination which can be studied elsewhere (see, for instance, Cuff et al., 1990).

functionalism

This perspective is also referred to as 'the society perspective' or the 'social system perspective'. It is a tradition of sociological thought that derives from the work of the French sociologist, Emile Durkheim, although it was principally given coherence by the American, Talcott Parsons (1902–79). In the early stages of the development of the discipline, in the 1940s to '60s, and particularly in the United States, it approximated a position of dominance. Today, following sustained criticism, there are few adherents amongst professional sociologists, but its importance lies in the enduring relevance of some aspects of the insights it generates and also in the similarities it shares with much commonsense thinking about social issues. It is for this reason, as Margaret Sargeant (1983) puts it, 'Talcott Parsons is dug up and reburied each year'.

Of the individual, the assumptions are pessimistic. Basic human nature is said to be self-centred and irrational. Society then acts as a civilising influence to make social order stable, orderly and harmonious; in effect preventing a Hobbesian 'war of all against all'. Society is more than the sum of its parts and confronts individuals as an object-ive reality. The relationship between the individual and society is then cast as a tension. The civilising influence of society keeps irrationality in check, with individuals not actively creating social lives but acting as products of the external society. Individuals can then only be free and happy within the confines set up by society. In this perspective there is an assumption of consensus on the basis of a shared system of values. This underlying assumption gives rise to statements such as, 'It's in the national interest', where there is assumed to be no conflict of interest. Social change is assumed to be only of a very gradual, evolutionary kind.

Within this perspective, *roles* provide the link between the individual and society in a fairly determinist fashion. As individuals we are linked to the various institutions of society by filling roles. At home, in the institution of kinship, we fill the roles of child or parent. At work, employer and employee. In the education system, pupil and teacher. In the health system, patient and health practitioner. Interaction between individuals is stabilised on the basis of a common value system; we agree on what should happen ('You want to get well, don't you?'). Conflict that may occur is to be understood as poor role performance. Divorce, for example, occurs because the partners are not fulfilling role requirements of husbands and wives adequately. In this perspective the process of *socialisation* is heavily emphasised. By being socialised we learn to be social, to keep our basically irrational tendencies in check, and we learn the content of role expectations. Divorce may also be caused by poor role socialisation. The solution is an idealist one: improve education for young people on how to be good husbands or wives.

Functionalism also uses the concept of *social systems* as the central unit of analysis. These social systems can range in scope from a *dyad* (a two-person social system, such as parent–child, teacher–pupil) up to the society as a whole. The key sense of sociological problem of this perspective is to ask, 'What is the function of a particular component of society, for example, religion, the family, universities, etc., in maintaining social order and the continued existence of society?'. Statements such as, 'Religion exists to sustain the moral foundations of society', are informed by this perspective. This is not the place to go into the drawbacks of the various perspectives, but it is important to note the assumption here is that society is *intended* to promote social order and integration.

The implication that 'society' can have a purpose or can be considered as an actor is called *reification*. In terms of logic, it should be noted it can result in a circular argument (called a *teleological* argument). In other words, our sociological bulsh detector should switch to red alert when we hear statements like, 'Society forces people to do . . .', or some reference to an unspecified 'they'. Statements like, 'Every society controls to a certain extent who may marry whom' (common in undergraduate essays), fail to consider who is actually doing the controlling or law making. The law makers and parliaments have decided you cannot marry your brother or sister, not some entity called society. Reification, while perhaps most common in functionalist accounts of social phenomena, is not restricted to that perspective, but is a more general alert. It occurs, for instance, whenever the term 'un-Australian' is used, which regrettably, seems to be occurring with increasing frequency in present political debate. Indeed, the respected social commentator Hugh McKay refers to it as 'an ugly word and a signpost to an ugly trend' (*The Age*, 20 June 2005).

conflict theories

This tradition may be understood as a set of theories and its most important figure is Karl Marx (1818–83), though many others are also involved. In discussing Marx's work we are separating (in a way Marx himself would have staunchly opposed) his analysis of society from his particular prescription of what should and would happen to change that society. Marx's work remains important to the social sciences despite attempts to discredit its relevance because of the collapse of societies in Eastern Europe and elsewhere based (albeit only very loosely) on his ideas.

In terms of the assumptions, conflict theories (of which, as with the other perspectives, there are a number) have a positive, optimistic view of human nature, arguing that human nature has been perverted by social arrangements through most of history. Society then is seen not as a civilising influence—as with functionalist theories—but as a corrupting influence, in effect creating conditions under which individuals become greedy, exploitative and uncooperative. In terms of the relationship between the individual and society, a key assumption is that conflict or coercion is the basis of a social order in which a minority of powerful people are able to impose their wills over the rest. (In the Marxian varieties of this perspective these groups of people are *classes*.) Unlike the functionalist perspective, then, conflict and conflicts of interest are a normal aspect of the way a society operates. Therefore, far from divorce being caused by poor role socialisation and performance, from this perspective, conflict is an endemic, normal part of a relationship. What happens, for instance, in a doctor's surgery is not assumed to be stabilised on the basis of shared values but may be the result of the patient and doctor sometimes having different outcome aims from the encounter. Rather than sharing the aim of getting well as quickly as possible, the patient may be more interested in securing a medical certificate to legitimate submitting an essay after the due date or getting time off work.

The relationship between the individual and society in this perspective is cast as a contradiction. People are the way they are because of the sort of society in which they live. Unlike functionalism, however, there exists the possibility that this contradiction can be resolved by changing the sort of society in which people live. Furthermore, this perspective makes a materialist assumption. The explanation for features of the society, such as inequality, conflict, change, unemployment, divorce etc., is to be sought in the way in which a particular society organises its economic life. The focus is on how economic production is organised. In the case of Australia and New Zealand, the term given to this organisation is 'capitalism', based on private ownership of resources and the production of goods and services for profit.

Hence amongst the terms 'advanced', 'modern', 'Western' and 'capitalist', which are used to describe what sort of society we live in, the last mentioned is the most important. Conflict theories tend to make quite determinist assumptions (and are frequently criticised for doing so). They are determinist in the sense that it is assumed that much of the shape of our society and many of its features are, to a greater or lesser extent (there's a lot of argument here, too), the result of the fact that we live in a capitalist society. These features not only include how education, health and other services are provided but also features such as the idea of fashionableness.

What else would convince you that it is time to spend some of your hard-earned money on new clothes when the ones you have are perfectly wearable—they are just not the new season's fashions!

The main differences between conflict theories and functionalism are the assumption of conflict in the former versus consensus in the latter, as well as how they view human nature and society. There are similarities, too: both are structural in orientation, articulating the relationship between the individual and society by beginning at the group level, then moving down to the individual level; both are objectivist in their view of society as having an independent existence; both are at least relatively determinist in focusing on society as a whole. The following example, however, should clarify how they differ and illustrate the implications of the different assumptions about the nature of the individual, of society, and of the relationship between the two.

One of the pleasures of visiting the beach is the feeling of warm sand under bare feet. The wisdom of seeking such pleasure, however, is under threat, at least in the larger coastal cities of Australia. This is because of the practice, made more poignant in the AIDS era, of intravenous drug users 'shooting up' on city beaches and then discarding their used needles or even deliberately planting them just below the surface of the sand, ready to cause a needlestick injury to the next bare foot that treads there. While there are thus far no reported cases of the transmission of the HIV virus as a result, a significant number of injuries have occurred, including many to children, so that it is no longer sensible to go barefooted on some famous city beaches, such as Bondi Beach in Sydney.

Two different ways of explaining such behaviour present themselves, related to the assumptions about the nature of the individual and society. One, functionalist in nature, would arise out of a pessimistic view of human nature, seeing the civilising effects of educating people in society as having failed to prevent such behaviour occurring. In other words, the primary responsibility for such behaviour lies at the individual level. The other way of understanding such behaviour, informed by conflict assumptions that are optimistic about human nature, would consider the way in which current social arrangements alienate and marginalise some groups of the population so that such behaviours may result. If it is likely that young people are responsible for such behaviour, then it is understandable in a time when a high proportion of young people are unemployed and more are likely to take an aggressive attitude to the safety of the rest of the community.

Since this is an aspect of the sociological imagination that is sometimes misunderstood, it is worth reiterating that holding the latter view does not absolve the people concerned from responsibility for their actions. Rather, it is to argue that we will not get far in stopping the practice by pursuing idealist (in the specific sociological sense of the term outlined earlier) solutions, by attempting to socialise and educate the people concerned not to engage in such antisocial practices. Instead, materialist solutions must be pursued, such as job creation and other means of integrating the perpetrators into the mainstream of social life from their position on the margins.

interactionism

As with conflict theories, this term refers to a tradition of theoretical approaches that have commonly arisen out of the microsociological work of the German sociologist Max Weber (1864–1920), although the approaches have been developed, particularly in the American context, by George Herbert Mead (1863–1931) and Alfred Schutz (1899–1959).

Weber's work spans both conflict theory and interactionism but interactionists, such as Mead and Schutz, used some of his understandings to develop their own approaches. This perspective is sometimes known as 'social action theory'. With its primary focus on small-scale social phenomena, this perspective tends to make relativistic assumptions about the nature of the individual, society and the relationship between the two: that they will vary with time and circumstance and are not absolute as the more objectivist perspectives of functionalism and conflict theory assume.

With this perspective, people are active agents, creating and recreating society rather than acting in accordance with some external constraints. It assumes individuals actively interpret in the sense of making sense of themselves, others and social and physical situations. From this perspective history has no grand design, either evolutionary or revolutionary. Events take place by the action of individuals collectively negotiating goals in the context of free will. Unlike the other perspectives there is little by way of a macro view of the world. Individuals act in terms of their interpretations to construct the group or societal level of interaction. As the sociological adage originating from the American sociologist W. I. Thomas states, 'That which is defined as real is real in its consequences', even in circumstances where those interpretations may be able to be demonstrated to be false. A neighbour of mine, for example, prefers not to paint his house too often as a means of discouraging burglars, hoping they will define the situation as, 'This is a house in which there is not likely to be much worth stealing'.

Interactionism then makes a subjectivist assumption that there is no absolute reality, but that people purposefully construct their social reality. The purpose is the goals they seek (such as not being burgled). Social action is assumed to be goal orientated. Individuals have free will to actively construct meaning in terms of their motivations.

This perspective is also idealist, according importance to ideas and values in the constructions of meaning that individuals make in their own right and not as derivative of some underlying objective material reality. No common system of values is assumed, unlike functionalism. Rather, the emphasis is on diversity of values as individuals try to achieve their goals which may be either in cooperation or in conflict with others. So interactionism makes different assumptions from either functionalism or conflict theory. In particular, it stresses free will rather than determinism and social life as subjective rather than objective reality. It shares with conflict theory the emphasis on conflict.

These perspectives represent the three main ways in which sociologists have conceptualised the relationship between the individual and society, which then provides the basis for their research practice. The perspectives differ according to the assumptions they make about some of the key debates in the philosophy of the social sciences. The philosophical differences result in different ways of understanding the nature of the sociological quest and also have an impact on the sense of sociological problem that each perspective addresses. The differences between the perspectives and the effect of the different philosophical assumptions on the sense of sociological problem that results, which therefore affects the sort of research undertaken, can be illuminated with an example.

an example—the sociology of death

The topic of death is perhaps not one that is obviously amenable to a sociological analysis, but from a sociological point of view we are interested in the fact that while the society as a whole continues to exist and survive over time, individual members 'turn up their toes' and pass out of that society. As indicated, functionalism concentrates on questions about the maintenance of a consensual social order. For sociologists from this perspective then (for example, Blauner, 1966), the sense of sociological problem that arises is how a society copes with the loss of individual members without the ongoing social order being unduly disrupted. The important question becomes, 'What is the function of death rituals, such as funerals, for the maintenance of social order?'. The answer is that these rituals help to mark the passing of an individual and assist those remaining to resume their function in society. Likewise, the convention and, indeed until recently, the legal requirement of mandatory retirement at age 65 in most jobs is functional for society because it minimises the disruption to the normal working of the society occasioned by having members of the society dying while holding important economic roles. Given that mandatory retirement has been challenged as discriminatory and ageist, the question from this point of view is, 'What will be the consequences for the maintenance of social order if this change occurs?'. Will it be functional for society to have people working on into their seventh and even eighth decades?

From a conflict perspective, the sorts of sociological questions that are asked concern the way in which the arrangements to do with death are organised, which is the result of the sort of society we live in (for example, Marcuse, 1972). Sociological accounts of death informed by a conflict perspective consider, for instance, the implications of the fact that we live in a capitalist society. Attention has therefore focused on the funeral industry and the way in which profitability is pursued in the marketing of various services that funeral companies offer (such as the variable price of coffins). Alternatively, studies may focus on what has come to be called the *commodification* of human services, in this case in the area of death and dying. With this sense of problem, sociologists find interesting, for instance, the Californian Yellow Pages®, where the range of services advertised includes being able to employ a suitably trained person to undertake 'the death watch'. For a reasonably hefty hourly rate, this person will sit with your relative or friend in the last hours before their death. In other words, in California you can pay for something which traditionally has been regarded as one of the most important kinship obligations. This is part of a general process identified by Marx: as capitalism develops, the cash nexus increasingly comes to replace the notion of personalised service. It becomes a commodity like anything else, to be bought and sold.

From an interactionist perspective, the key sorts of sociological questions asked differ again. Accounts based on this perspective consider the way in which social action occurs as individual members of society imbue with meaning the death of one of their number. The focus here is not on the broader society and how it structures the experience of dying for individuals, but more upon smaller-scale interaction within hospitals, funeral parlours, etc. Operating from this perspective, sociologists might consider the way a language has evolved which is 'deathless' ('passing on' rather than 'dying', 'deceased' rather than 'dead', 'interred' rather than 'buried', a 'floral tribute' rather than 'flowers'). Altern-atively, they may consider the routines and procedures that have evolved in hospital settings to minimise the disruptive impact of individual patients dying (such as a special elevator to the morgue to remove the need for visitors to share the lift with a corpse). Or they might study the different definitions of the situation held by health workers for whom death is routine and commonplace, and the rest of us for whom it is not. This tension is ably reflected in the supposedly true story of a medical student, who was very nearly expelled from medical school after he leaned out of the window of an anatomy laboratory and inquired of the window cleaner working there whether he would like a hand! Alternatively, they may study, as Allan Kellehear (1990) did in his classic work in this field, the manner in which the notion of 'good death' is constructed.

Of course, the sense of problem raised by all three perspectives are relevant sociological questions in understanding the phenomenon of death in society. The point is that the perspective from which the researcher operates will affect the sorts of sociological problems that are considered to be relevant, as well as how the researcher goes about investigating that phenomenon.

Several other points are relevant to the example of the different sociological perspectives on death used above. First, all sociological accounts are informed by perspectives. The unity of theory and method is what makes sociology distinctive. It is not possible to have a perspectiveless account of social phenomena, only degrees of implicitness and explicitness. All sociological analysis operates from a particular perspective, in the sense of providing a basis from which analysis can proceed, even if that perspective is only implicit in the author's account. This relates to the argument in the previous chapter about the question of values, where it was argued that a value-free account was impossible. Even to decide what sorts of sociological questions to ask about a particular phenomenon requires taking some sort of position in relation to the underlying philosophical debates which inform the perspectives. Most sociologists would argue that it is preferable to be reasonably explicit about the perspective from which one operates.

Second, it relates to the question of critique, which I have argued is an essential component of the quest for sociological understanding. One can be critical of another's account of an aspect of the social world in two ways: either in terms of the conventional criteria of the adequacy of the empirical evidence or data used to support the argument (which I shall deal with in the next section); or in terms of a different perspective taken to inform one's account of the particular topic. For instance, one might be critical of an interactionist account of the social processes that surround death on the (more structuralist) grounds that they fail to adequately take account of the broader context in which the services surrounding the death of an individual are organised on a business basis. Likewise, from an interactionist perspective, one may be critical of more structural accounts for failing to take adequate account of the interactional details and for assuming that what actually occurs will be determined by the broader societal level considerations.

Third, there is the often-asked question of the extent to which one can mix the perspectives to suit the purpose in hand; sometimes called a *pluralist perspective*. The answer to this question has to be that it is possible to some extent. A sociological analysis of death is improved by taking into consideration the sorts of insights generated by all three perspectives outlined in the example above. The limitation on a sort of theoretical smorgasbord, however, comes from the underlying philosophical bases. The positions that are taken by the different perspectives are at times mutually incompatible. One cannot assume both an optimistic and pessimistic view of human nature. At a philosophical level they may be what is called *incommensurable*.

Finally, we can consider how the earlier chapters of this book relate to the idea of perspectives—how the sociological imagination, arising from exercising sensibilities towards the historical, cultural, structural and critical aspects of sociological analysis, is incorporated into a sociological understanding, for instance of death, will depend on the perspective taken. So, taking a historical sensibility as the example, if you operate within a functionalist perspective then the relevant historical issues to consider will be the history of retirement policy or changes in the format of funerals, for example. If, however, your social analysis is informed by a conflict perspective, then the relevant historical questions will include the history of the funeral parlour industry, its origins as a sideline for furniture makers and the gradual emergence of it as a specialised service industry. Incorporating a cultural sensibility from a functionalist perspective will focus on how funeral rituals are performed in different cultures or how retirement policy is organised elsewhere. From a conflict perspective, the relevant question might be something like, 'Is the Californian example given above something specific to west-coast American culture, or is it a consequence of the more general process of commodification such that this service will eventually appear in Yellow Pages® telephone books in Wellington or Perth as well?'. From an interactionist perspective, the appropriate question might be how to make practices surrounding the dead (in hospitals or funeral homes) more culturally sensitive to different ethnic groups, in line with their particular beliefs and customs. In other words, the quest for sociological understanding requires these sensibilities to be built into social analysis, but how and the extent to which it is done will depend to a considerable extent on the perspective taken.

how do we know?

As indicated earlier in the chapter the different perspectives can be differentiated in two main ways. The assumptions they make in regard to key debates in the philosophy of the social sciences is the first. The other is in terms of the answer given to the epistemological question of, 'How can we know the social world?'; that is, about the status of the knowledge to be derived from the various perspectives. The last section of this chapter will consider this question.

The perspective taken has implications for how we do sociology and what we consider to be its subject matter. This is the link between the theoretical or non-observable aspects of the social world and the empirical or observable aspects. In other words, it is to discuss the relationship between concepts you cannot see (such as class), and those you can see (such as education levels). Empirical research about the social world does not occur in a vacuum; rather, it is conducted within a particular perspective. These relate closely to the approaches to the discipline itself outlined in an earlier chapter. There a distinction was drawn between the approach to the discipline usually called positivism, which sees sociology as emulating the natural and physical sciences, and the non-positivist approach, sometimes called naturalism, which sees the social sciences as different from the natural and physical sciences and which therefore pursues the sociological quest differently. Having considered the underlying assumptions, we are now in a position to understand better the difference between these two approaches to the nature of the discipline and then relate it to the perspectives outlined above.

The crucial assumption concerns the nature of reality. Objectivist approaches assume a definite social reality exists. Subjectivist approaches, by contrast, assume people give meaning to a social setting, and thus socially construct a reality. Positivist approaches assume an objectivist reality, therefore one can *know by measuring*. If a social reality exists out there, then the sociologist operating from this perspective can emulate their natural and physical science colleagues and take their version of the thermometer or the Geiger counter, which is most likely to be a questionnaire, into a particular social setting to know what is happening there; in other words, to research it. Sociologists operating within this positivist tradition therefore have a preference for what is usually called *quantitative* methods of gathering data over other methods.

Sociologists operating within the non-positivist tradition of doing sociology, however, seek to know things about the social world in a different manner. Arising from a subjectivist assumption about the nature of reality, these sociologists pursue their sociological quest by seeking to *know by interpreting or understanding*. If social reality is constructed by participants pursuing their goals, then the sociologist must try to tap into the meaning the participants give to the social settings of which they are a part. The epistemological process is called *verstehen* (pronounced 'ver-shtay-en'). This German word, coined by Max Weber, expresses an idea that cannot easily be translated into the English language. It means interpretively understanding the actions of others by putting yourself in their place to see the meaning they attach to social action, as well as what their goals are. This methodological approach to the question of how we can know things about the social world favours certain *qualitative* methods, such as observation, over others. An example may make this distinction clearer.

Consider the social setting within educational institutions known as the tutorial or class. If we started out wanting to know what happened within a particular tutorial setting, the two approaches outlined above would approach the question in different ways. Within the positivist tradition with its objectivist assumption, the preferred method for knowing what occurred within that setting would be to administer a questionnaire to participants on their perceptions of what was occurring. A sociologist operating within a qualitative, non-positivist tradition would probably seek to know what was occurring by sitting in the tutorial, observing the nature of the interaction and then interpretively understanding the meaning of what they saw (students nodding off, etc.). Each sociologist would seek to understand, but would do their sociology in a different way. Both are legitimate ways of doing research but they are based on different epistemological traditions. In other words, the method chosen to investigate a subject arises out of a particular perspective.

The link between the perspective taken and the method used to gather data about the social world is clearly an important one. In terms of the particular perspectives of functionalism, conflict theory and interactionism outlined above, the more structuralist accounts of functionalism and conflict theory tend, broadly speaking, to operate within a positivist tradition while the interactionist perspective clearly operates within a non-positivist tradition using the methodology of *verstehen*.

conclusion

This chapter considered the idea of perspectives within sociology. These perspectives are sociological representations of the underlying philosophical debates of the social sciences. The three perspectives outlined—functionalism, interactionism and conflict theory—represent the main theoretical traditions within which the sociological quest may proceed. Another way of saying this is that these are, to a greater or lesser extent, the main traditions within which sociology is practised today. Flowing from the perspective taken will be a preference for certain methods of doing sociology over others. In other words, there is a fundamental unity in the discipline between theory and method.

Sociological analysis then has as its fundamental feature a concern with relating the unobservable aspects of the social world to the observable. The unobservable is the social theory that underlies the discipline. The observable is evidence about the social world. Sociology cannot be practised without the existence of both.

8 doing sociology

This final chapter will consider some practical aspects of the sociological quest, in particular what it means for the person engaged in the quest for sociological understanding. It is relatively uncommon for academic books to address this question explicitly, but it is relevant to the view of the discipline presented in this short book.

What are the prerequisites for embarking on the quest for sociological understanding? According to Ruggiero (1996: 5) there are three minimum requirements which appear to be, but are not, self-evident:

First, you should be curious about issues and willing to invest the time and energy necessary to find the most accurate and complete answers to your questions. Second, you should already have, or be willing to adopt, the habit of evaluating ideas on the basis of evidence rather than on the basis of whether they agree with your current prior opinions or the current intellectual fashion. Finally, you should be aware of the limitations of your knowledge and willingness to learn from others. That doesn't mean you must accept everything you read or hear. On the contrary, the aim . . . is to help you think independently, as all good sociologists do, selecting worthy issues for analysis, asking penetrating questions, consulting available research (in some cases conducting your own research), reaching sound conclusions, and presenting your ideas persuasively.

In learning about a new area of study, there are two separate aspects involved: those of content and process. Both are involved in developing what are called *competencies*. *Content* refers to what is actually learned, the specific content of information about the subject in question. These are work-related competencies that in some tertiary training provide the basis for employment in a professional field. Learning how to bandage a sprained ankle is a work-related competency that forms part of the education of nurses, for instance. Probably the most important work-related competency offered in a tertiary degree in sociology is research skill: the ability to conduct research and analyse the empirical data, both quantitative and qualitative, which results from that research.

Process, by contrast, refers to how you learn it; the more generic skills by which the content is imparted and developed. These are more knowledge-based competencies that involve problem solving and effective communication, such as knowing how to use libraries properly to access material effectively, how to summarise and distil the main arguments being made, how to organise ideas effectively and make cogent arguments. Tertiary training should be seen as an opportunity not only to learn about particular disciplines but also to develop the sorts of process skills important to capitalising on the advantageous position in the labour market that being a graduate entails.

By the end of a tertiary training in sociology, all students should aim to have developed such competencies as having excellent keyboard skills, knowing how to use electronic databases in the field (especially sociological abstracts), knowing how to surf the World Wide Web (and separate the 'wheat from the chaff' educationally speaking), as well as being able to track down the sources of reports appearing in print and other media. Educational programs, particularly at tertiary level, tend to focus mainly on the content aspect of pedagogy. Process skills are expected to be picked up along the way. Yet it is the academic process skills that are retained from a tertiary education long after the specific content of particular disciplines is forgotten. Furthermore, studies have shown that it is these competencies that employers are frequently most interested in with graduates of more generalist degrees (see Marginson, 1993). In this chapter some of the process aspects involved in doing sociology are considered. Of course, not all of these are specific to sociology itself but are shared with other disciplines, particularly with other social science disciplines.

This book has been designed to introduce the reader to the discipline of sociology, particularly as it is currently practised in Australasia. What has been referred to as the quest for sociological understanding is the start of a process that for many will lead them to including at least an introductory subject in the discipline at tertiary level. These subjects may be either designed as a service course in the context of professional studies in some other area, or an introductory course in themselves. Such subjects, for which this book will serve as an introduction, usually have specific aims. These aims do not usually include training students in a mass of facts about the society in which they live or other detailed content. Rather, they more often attempt to impart process skills about the discipline itself, embarking students on the quest for sociological understanding and helping to develop the beginnings of an ability to have a sociological imagination.

Subsequent years of study beyond the introductory level will hone and develop this quest through many of the interesting empirical or substantive areas of sociological specialisation.

For many, the quest is a limited one, gaining a sense of sociological perspective in professional training courses such as nursing. For others, it may be adding a sociology subject to a degree in some other major field of study, such as psychology or history. In some cases, the quest is pursued to the level of a whole tertiary degree in the subject, where it then often becomes the basis and background for more specialised development of work-related competencies, such as vocationally oriented postgraduate study in, for example, teaching or social work, to name only a couple. For others still, it continues with specialised postgraduate study in sociology itself and the attainment of at least a fourth-year qualification (such as 'honours') after which (and only after which) the occupational designation 'sociologist' is appropriate, with employment then pursued in a wide variety of fields.

The process of developing a sociological imagination involves detailed and sustained study, usually in a variety of different fields of the discipline as the ability to 'think sociologically' is honed and refined over time. It cannot, it is worth saying, be developed by taking a crash course in sociological methods. This will not develop a sociological imagination any more than a knowledge of the properties of building materials, such as wood, concrete and steel, will make an architect.

This book is oriented to the introductory level; to introduce students to sociology and hopefully challenge them to develop a sociological imagination. At this basic level, the pedagogical aim is to help students to begin to do certain things: to *think* in sociological terms about the society in which they live; to *understand* sociologically such features of that society as social structures, relationships, meanings and situations; and to *explain* these by using the theories and methods of the discipline.

In order to do this, the teaching of introductory subjects attempts to get students to understand something of the complexity of society, to realise that many of the aspects of society are somewhat more complex than they may have realised. It is as if they have been afloat on the lake of society for however many years they have lived. The teaching of the subject helps them to look into the lake to see what keeps them afloat. Taking a subject like sociology often raises more questions than it answers in that the process of being educated is learning to understand one's own ignorance about the world. This quest also encourages the seeker not to take the social world for granted, but to be reflexive or critical about its nature and the place of the individual within it. This aim has particular implications. Studying sociology is often different from studying other subjects. Other subjects may be left in the classroom at the end of the day, but sociology by its very nature cannot be left in this way. For instance, the example developed in the last chapter concerning the different perspectives on death probably set the reader thinking and reflecting on the social processes surrounding the death of someone close to them. Likewise, travelling in elevators may never be the same again!

Being reflexive about the social world and one's place in it can be personally challenging as it doubts and undermines the taken-for-granted understanding that an individual has developed. If there is one central premise on which all sociologists would agree it is that, when it comes to the social world, things are rarely what they seem. There are complexities and layers of meaning that are quickly uncovered. The act of examining the social world can result in one questioning the understandings developed about the nature of the society in which one lives. For instance, it may be comforting to believe that there is little poverty in society or that those who occupy the bottom rungs of society are there as a result of their own actions in not staying at school long enough or whatever. It is frequently challenging to read about and come to understand the growth in and extent of, for example, income inequality in society.

Alternatively, it may be interesting to read about the AIDS pandemic, but some of the research might be considered a 'bit close to home'. Turtle et al. (1989), for instance, surveyed the AIDS-related beliefs and behaviours of Australian university students. Their findings first reported as long ago as 1989, but since reproduced among many other groups in society, are disturbing. Although students understood very well what causes the transmission of the HIV virus and knew what to do to prevent transmission, they were not actually translating that knowledge into action by practising safe sex (specifically using condoms in their sexual relationships) in great numbers. The gap between knowledge and attitudes on the one hand and practice on the other (what has become known as the 'KAP gap'—knowledge, attitudes, practice), is a major challenge facing health educators in attempting to control the spread of the virus. Furthermore, the KAP gap is found even amongst the most educated group of young people in society, those at the stage of their lives in forming relationships when they may be vulnerable to transmission of the virus. Studying sociology, therefore, can be quite confronting to one's own understanding of the social world.

At the same time, the quest for sociological understanding of the social world does not come from textbooks and tutorial discussions alone. It is also based importantly upon experience. Like sex, sociology is much more fun to do than to read about or talk about! The quest involves an active curiosity about social settings and situations. This does not serve, it should be noted, to legitimate the occasional caricature of the sociologist eavesdropping and keyhole watching. But it does enjoin students of the social organisation of society to actively inquire into the social settings of which they are a part. Part of the sociological quest is to observe, ask, interpret and reflect on what is occurring, as well as on the traditional sociological question of the place of the individual in the larger scheme of things.

C. Wright Mills, in his famous appendix to *The Sociological Imagination* (1959) entitled 'On Intellectual Craftsmanship', suggests the keeping of a journal in which these observations, reflections and interpretations can be recorded. According to Ruggiero (1996: 49) a journal can be useful as:

> . . . a record of ideas that are in themselves interesting and thus seem to merit closer inspection—you write them down—so that you can reflect on them later . . . To keep a journal, you first capture ideas and then, usually at a later time, reflect on their meaning and value.

This reflection extends to one's own social location, and the extent to which one's own experience is typical or atypical of others similarly located in society. It often comes as a shock to students to realise that their experience is less common than they had always assumed. Knowledge, after all, is possible on grounds other than personal experience; one does not have to be able to play a violin to recognise a bad note, or to have been to South Africa during the apartheid period to understand racism for that matter. Personal experience is a relevant and important part of the answer to the question, 'How can we know things about the social world?', but students are often surprised to realise, on studying the relevant research, that their own personal experience of social life is less able to be generalised to others than they thought. 'Commonsense', on careful examination, often turns out to be less common and to make less sense than had been assumed. Coming to terms with the more specialised language of sociology is therefore important to the sociological quest as a means of facilitating this understanding. For this reason, a crucial tool in the quest is a specialised sociology dictionary such as Jary and Jary (1991) or Turner (2006).

The extent to which we can know what is happening in our society and how it is changing on the basis of personal experience is relatively limited. For this reason we are dependent on other sources of evidence to inform our understanding. Personal experience is one means of informing us about what is happening, another is the media: radio, television and especially high-quality newspapers. Regular reading and watching news and current affairs programs is an essential part of the quest for sociological understanding. Of course, such evidence about the social world must be approached critically; some of the information presented is much more reliable than the rest. Likewise, the internet must be approached critically as a medium (that is, one type of media) that, like other media, will have material of varying usefulness. A couple of examples will help explain this point further.

Amongst the least reliable sources of evidence regarding, for instance, public opinion about a particular issue, are the polls frequently conducted by television stations—where those watching are invited to record their support or opposition for a particular issue by ringing a particular phone number. On occasions I have received urgent email requests from organisations to which I belong, asking their membership to participate in one of these polls. These are then reported by the media organisation concerned as if they somehow represent public opinion on a particular matter. Much more reliable—though still partial—understanding can be gained from the results of public opinion polls properly conducted by polling organisations. The act of being critical about this as a source of information is in terms of the particular ways in which.questions may be asked. One example asked respondents in a telephone survey whether they thought the level of state assistance (the money paid in subsidies) to private schools should be increased or decreased. For those who think the state should not fund private schools at all, an answering option that would reflect their opinion was not available.

The most reliable sources of information about the society in which we live are the major surveys of the state of the nation, such as the 2006 census in Australia. From the census results, a picture is gradually emerging of the state of the nation and the way in which it is changing. Such information needs to be reflected upon and interpreted. What does it mean that the Anglo-Celtic ethnic dominance of Australian society is gradually being eroded, with each successive census showing a greater and greater proportion of the Australian population recording an ethnic background other than an Anglo-Celtic one? What will it mean for a future Federal Republic of Australasia when, by the second decade of this century, the proportion of elderly people will have doubled? What social policy challenges will face the important policy makers of tomorrow, many of whom may now be reading this book and starting their tertiary education careers? What sort of environmental legacy will this generation of policy makers and the next bestow upon their children and grandchildren in the era of climate change?

Yet even the census needs to be approached critically insofar as it is able to answer these sorts of questions. Scepticism is needed to interpret the broader underlying processes by which societies are changing. An example is the debate about whether Australia is becoming a more secular society. As sociologists we are interested in the process of secularisation (the social process by which organised religion has less influence over everyday life). The decline of the Sabbath (Sunday) as a day of religious observance is one example. Shops, bars and restaurants are open, sporting events and house auctions are commonplace; all are evidence it can be argued, of secularisation. The author recalls visiting the protestant areas of East Belfast in Northern Ireland in the 1980s where the swings in children's playgrounds were chained up on a Sunday so they could not be used!

Yet the census data on religious adherence is perhaps not very helpful in understanding this phenomenon. This is because of what might be called the ongoing, if perhaps declining, social acceptability of entering some religious affiliation when filling out the census rather than 'none'. Because of social mores, people may still claim a religious affiliation even though it may have been many years since they actually attended a religious service (if ever!), other than for what the French anthropologist Levi Strauss called the 'rites de passage'. These rites of passage or life changes (the 'hatching, matching, and despatching'; or christenings, marriages and funerals), have traditionally been the core of religious activities. Instead, their significance has been replaced by more secular rites of passage such as graduation from university. Because of this social phenomenon of secularisation, while the census can reveal, for instance, the relative decline in traditional Christian churches and the concomitant growth in 'new age' and non-Christian religions, it is less useful in enabling us to understand the evidence for the extent of the social process of secularisation. And it is even less useful in understanding the not insignificant numbers of Australians who record their religious affiliation as 'Jedi Knight'!

Fortunately though, other sources of information from the census do speak to the growth of a secular society. If established religion once had a virtual monopoly on the 'matching' ritual in society (weddings), then this has certainly changed. When the ABS compares the number of marriage ceremonies conducted by ministers of religion on one hand and civil marriage celebrants on the other, it was in 1999 that the numbers of secular 'matchings' overtook religious ones and their growth has continued since so that civil ceremonies in 2008 accounted for 65 per cent of all marriages (ABS, 2009). Likewise the census data records those behaviours that were once heavily proscribed (if not forbidden) by established religions such as couples living together before they had 'tied the knot'. In 2008, 77 per cent of all couples indicated they had lived together before marriage (ABS 2009).

Another Australian example is the habitation of the Murray-Darling Basin, occupying more than a million square kilometres, or one-seventh of the total area of Australia, and home to Aboriginal communities for more than 40 000 years. In the era of climate change, if current patterns of the social organisation of settlement and land usage continue, it is possible that much of this area might become unfit for habitation due to increasing salination of the land.

Personal experience and the media are sources of information about the social world that together with socio-logical research information (and other research from other disciplines) provide the basis for understanding society. It is the sociological research about our societies that students will spend most of their time studying, at least in the early stages of their education in sociology. Fortunately, the sociological study of Australian and New Zealand society has progressed to the point where we are no longer reliant upon research generated about other societies. Likewise, we are no longer reliant on textbooks written about northern hemisphere societies to assist in this quest. Instead of learning about sociology via the study of kinship patterns in London, or race relations in American cities, we are now able to pursue the quest by studying social issues in this part of the world, such as black power gangs in Auckland, Italian settlers in the Riverina district in Victoria, company mining towns in Queensland, and relations between neighbours in Melbourne or Wellington suburbs. Ably assisted by such organisations as the Australian Institute of Family Studies, the Australian Institute of Health and Welfare, the Australian Youth Research Centre and the Australian Research Centre for Sex, Health and Society, the extent of our understanding of the society in which we live has enormously increased.

The sociological quest is not only an intellectual one, but also a personal one. Studying the relationship between the individual and society, building a historical, cultural, structural and critical awareness, is ultimately to reflect on your place, as an individual, in the larger scheme of things. Reflexivity, self-awareness and a critical understanding of your own society at this point in history are all part of the process of what it means to be educated. For Wright Mills (1959: 104), educated people are those who are 'imaginatively aware of their own sensibilities and capable of continuous self-cultivation'. Sociology alone, of course, does not provide this complete understanding, but sociology has an important place in the process.

Finally, the view of the discipline of sociology that I have presented in this book is a fairly practical one. The sociological imagination involves not only seeking to understand the social world and how it operates but also, as Giddens (1983) has argued, to assess what sorts of social change are desirable and feasible and how to achieve those changes. For Wright Mills (1959: 226) it involves, 'a chance to make a difference to the quality of human life in our time'. The social policy questions remain central: questions such as, 'How can we achieve the social conditions for the maximum realisation of human potentiality?'. Sociology involves the search for these alternative futures, for what might be, as well as for what is. Ultimately such is the goal of the sociological quest.

bibliography

Altius Directory, 2010, <www.altiusdirectory.com/Sports/ 2010-wimbledon-tennis-prize-money.php> [21 May 2010]

Amato, P. 1993, 'Children's adjustment to divorce: Theories, hypotheses, and empirical support', *Journal of Marriage and Family*, vol. 55, pp. 23–38

Andersson, N., Ho-Foster, A., Mitchell, S., Scheepers, E., and Goldstein, S. 2007, 'Risk factors for domestic physical violence: National cross-sectional household surveys in eight southern African countries', *BMC Women's Health*, vol. 7, no. 11 <www.biomedcentral.com/1472–6874/7/11> [23 May 2010]

Armstrong, S. 1991, 'Female circumcision: Fighting a cruel tradition', *New Scientist*, 2 February, pp. 22–7

Atkinson, A. and Leigh, A. 2005, 'The distribution of top incomes in Australia and New Zealand', ANU Discussion Paper No. 514

Austin, D. 1984, *Australian Sociologies*, Allen & Unwin, Sydney

Australian Automobile Association, 2003, 'Australian new car assessment program', <www.aaa.asn.au/NCAP/ozindex. htm> [29 April 2010]

Ausfood, 2009, 'Chocolate resilient, seafood sales buoyant as Easter sales entice food spending', media release <www.ausfoodnews.com.au/2009/04/09/chocolate-resilient-seafood-sales-buoyant-as-easter-sales-entice-food-spending.html> [6 May 2010]

Australian Bureau of Statistics, 1993, *Social Atlas of Melbourne*, Canberra

——1994, *Focus on Families: Demographics and Family Formation*, Canberra

——2000, *Australian Social Trends 1997: Family-Living Arrangements: One-parent families*, Canberra

——2000b, *Australian Social Trends 1999: Family Formation: Remarriage trends of divorced people*, Canberra

——2001, *Indigenous Health: Greater Risks, Shorter Life Expectancy*, cat. no. 4704.0, Canberra

——2002, *Births, Australia*, cat. no. 3301.0, Canberra.

——2003, *Yearbook Australia: population, births*, Canberra

——2006, *Deaths, Australia*, cat. no. 3302.0

——2007, *Australian Social Trends*, cat. no. 4102.0

——2009, *Marriages and Divorces, Australia, 2008*, cat. no. 3310.0, Canberra

Australian Medical Association (AMA), 2001, 'Forty per cent drop in GP's delivering babies' <www.ama.com.au/node/815 Press release 12th May

AUSVEG (Vegetable Industry Development Program), 2010, 'Quarterly report reveals men like it hot', media release, 5 May <www.ausveg.com.au/news.cfm?CID=7423> [22 May 2010]

Barker-Benfield, B. 1972, *Horrors of the Half-known Life*, Harper Torchbooks, New York

Baum, F. 1998, 'Private grief to public troubles: Suicide and public health', *In Touch: Newsletter of the Public Health Association of Australia*, February, p. 3

Beck, U. and Beck-Gernsheim E., 2002, *Individualization: institutionalized individualism and its social and political consequences*, Sage, London

Berger, P. 1963, *An Invitation to Sociology*, Penguin, New York

Bittman, M. 2004, 'Parenthood without penalty: Time use and public policy in Australia and Finland' in Bittman, M. & Folbre, N. (eds), *Family Time: The Social Organization of Care*, Routledge London/New York, pp. 224–43

Blauner, R. 1966, 'Death and the social structure', *Psychiatry*, vol. 29, no. 4, pp. 378–94

Boyle, P., Gandini, S. and Gray, N. 2008, 'Epidemiology of lung cancer: A century of great success and ignominious failure' in Hansen, H. (ed) *Textbook of Lung Cancer*, 2nd edn, pp. 10–19

Burns, A., Bottomley, G. and Jools, P. (eds), 1983, *The Family in the Modern World*, Allen & Unwin, Sydney

Callan, V. 1986, *Australian Minority Groups*, HBJ, Sydney

Centre for Disease Control, 2007, 'United States unintentional firearm deaths and rates per 100,000', Atlanta <http://webappa.cdc.gov/cgi-bin/broker.exe> [15 June 10]

Chalmers, A. 1982, *What is This Thing Called Science?*, 2nd edn, University of Queensland Press, St Lucia

Chronicle of the Olympics, 1998, 2nd edn, DK Publishing, London

Coggan, C., Disley, B., Patterson, P. and Norton, R. 1997, 'Risk-taking behaviours in a sample of New Zealand adolescents', *Australian and New Zealand Journal of Public Health*, vol. 21, no. 5, pp. 455–62

Collins, R. 1982, *Sociological Insight: An introduction to non-obvious sociology*, Oxford University Press, New York

Confectionery Manufacturers Association, 2003, 'Chocolate festival in the confectionery calendar set to get bigger' <www.candy.net.au/cma/components/news/archive_article.asp?id=180> [29 May 2010]

Coulson, M. and Riddell, D. 1970, *Approaching Sociology: A critical introduction*, Routledge, London

Cuff, E., Sharrock, W. and Francis, D. 1990, *Perspectives in Sociology*, 3rd edn, Unwin Hyman, London

DatabaseOlympics.com, 2010, <www.databaseolympics.com> [2 June 2010]

De Vaus, D. and Wolcott, I. (eds), 1997, *Australian Family Profiles*, Australian Institute of Family Studies, Melbourne

De Visser, R., Smith, A., Rissel, C., Richters, J., Crulich, A. 2003, 'Sex in Australia: Safer sex and condom use among a representative sample of adults', *Australian and New Zealand Journal of Public Health*, vol. 27, no. 2, pp. 223–9

Durkheim, E. 1970, *Suicide: A study in sociology*, Routledge and Kegan Paul, London

Eades, D. 1985, 'You gotta know how to talk . . . information seeking in south east Queensland Aboriginal society', J. Pride (ed.), *Cross Cultural Communication: Communication and mis-Communication*, River Seine Publications, Melbourne

Elliott, J. R., and Pais, J. 2006, 'Race, class, and Hurricane Katrina: Social differences in human responses to disaster', *Social Science Research*, vol. 35, no. 2, pp. 295–321

Family Law Council, 1994, 'Female genital mutilation: Discussion paper', 31 January, Canberra

Federal Chamber of Automotive Industries, 2009, 'New vehicle market', <www.fcai.com.au/sales/new-vehicle-market> [6 June 2010]

Foucault, M. 1974, 'Michel Foucault on Attica', interview, *Telos*, Spring, pp. 154–61

Freidson, E. 1986, *Professional Powers: A study of the institutionalisation of formal knowledge*, University of Chicago Press, Chicago.

Furze, B. 2008, 'Environmental Sustainability' in Furze, B., Savy, P., Brym, R. and Lie, J. (eds), *Sociology in Today's World*, Cengage, Melbourne, pp. 538–57

Game, A. 1991, *Undoing the Social: Towards a deconstructive sociology*, Open University Press, Milton Keynes

Giddens, A. 1983, *Sociology: A brief but critical introduction*, MacMillan, London

——1991, *Modernity and Self Identity: Self and society in the late modern age*, Polity Press, Cambridge

Goldthorpe, J. C. 1974, *An Introduction to Sociology*, Cambridge University Press, London

Gould, S. 1981, *The Mismeasure of Men*, Norton, New York

Gouldner, A., 1973, 'Anti-minotaur: The myth of a value-free sociology' in Gouldner, A. (ed.), *For Sociology: Renewal and critique in sociology today*, Allen Lane, London

Graduate Careers Council of Australia (GCCA), 1992, *Graduate Destination Survey 1991*, GCCA, Melbourne

Gray, N. 1995, 'Perceptions of the contemporary status of smoking control strategies', *Australian Journal of Public Health*, vol. 19, no. 2, pp. 116–20

Hamblin, J. 1994, 'HIV, law and ethics in developing countries', *Australian Health Law Bulletin*, vol. 2, no. 1, pp. 71–2

Harriss, J. 2000. 'The second great transformation? Capitalism at the end of the twentieth century' in *Poverty and Development into the 21st Century*, revised edition, Allen, T. and Thomas, A. (eds), Oxford University Press Oxford, pp. 325–42

Hubbard, R., and Wald, E. 1993, *Exploding the Gene Myth*, Beacon Press, Boston

Jary, D., and Jary, J. 1991, *Collins Dictionary of Sociology*, Harper Collins, Glasgow

Jolly, H. 1983, *Commonsense About Babies and Children*, Unwin, London

Kellehear, A. 1990, *Dying of Cancer*, Harwood, London

Kinsey, A., Pomeroy, W. and Martin, C. 1948, *Sexual Behavior in the Human Male*, Saunders, Philadelphia

——1953, *Sexual Behavior in the Human Female*, Saunders, Philadelphia

Koch, H. 1985, 'Non-standard English in an Aboriginal land claim', in J. Pride (ed.), *Cross Cultural Communication: Communication and mis-Communication*, River Seine Publications, Melbourne

Koenig, M. and D'Sousa, S. 1986, 'Sex differences in childhood mortality in Bangladesh', *Social Science and Medicine*, vol. 22, pp. 15–22

Laumann, E., Michael, S., Michael, R. and Gagnon, J. 1994, *The Social Organization of Sexuality*, Chicago University Press, Chicago

Leigh A. and Anderson, A. 2010, The distribution of top incomes in five anglo-saxon countries over the twentieth century, IZA Discussion Paper No. 4937 [May 2010] people.anu.edu.au/andrew.leigh/pdf/TopIncomesAnglo.pdf [10 June 2010]

Little, G. 1974, 'The Sandclasses', in D. Edgar (ed.), *Social Change in Australia: Readings in Sociology*, Cheshire, Melbourne, pp. 249–51

Marcuse, H. 1972, *Eros and Civilisation*, Abacus, London

Marginson, S. 1993, *Arts, Science and Work: Work-related skills and the generalist courses in higher education*, Australian Government Publishing Service (AGPS), Canberra

Mathews, J. 1985, *Health and Safety at Work: A trade union safety representative's handbook*, Pluto Press, Leichhardt

Mead, M. 1930, *Coming of Age in Samoa*, Morrow, New York

Mouer, R. and Sugimoto, Y. 1986, *Images of Japanese Society: a Study in the Social Construction of Reality*, KPI, London

National Occupational Health and Safety Commission, 1996, *Compendium of Workers' Compensation Statistics, Australia, 1994–95*, National and Workplace Statistics and Epidemiology Branch, AGPS, Canberra

O'Malley, P. 1975, 'Suicide and war', *British Journal of Criminology*, vol. 15, no. 4, pp. 348–59

O'Neill, J. 2009, *The Irish Potato Famine*, ABDO, Minnesota

Orange, C. 1989, *The Story of a Treaty*, Allen & Unwin, Wellington

Prus, R. and Dawson, L. 1991, 'Shop till you drop: shopping as recreational and laborious behaviour', *Canadian Journal of Sociology*, vol. 16, no. 2, pp. 145–64

Quinlan, M. and Bohle, P. 1991, *Managing Occupational Health and Safety in Australia: A multidisciplinary approach*, MacMillan, South Melbourne

Raskall, P. 1978, 'Who's got what in Australia: the distribution of wealth', *Journal of Australian Political Economy*, no. 2, pp. 3–16

Robertson, I. 1987, *Sociology*, 3rd edn, Worth, New York

Rose, S., Lewontin, R. and Kamin, L. 1984, *Not in Our Genes: Biology, ideology and human nature*, Penguin, London

Ruggiero, V. R. 1996, *A Guide to Sociological Thinking*, Sage, Thousand Oaks, California

Sargeant, M. 1983, *Sociology for Australians*, Longman Cheshire, Melbourne

Sen, A. 1992, 'Missing women: Social inequality outweighs women's survival advantage in Asia and North Africa', *British Medical Journal*, vol. 304, March, pp. 587–8

Shilling, C. 2003, *The Body and Social Theory*, Sage, London

Simmel, G. 1959, 'The Stranger', in Wolff, K. (ed.), *Georg Simmel, 1858–1918: A collection of essays*, Ohio University Press, Columbus

Singer, P. 1993, *How Are We to Live: Ethics in an age of self-interest*, Text Publishing, Melbourne

Smith-Rosenberg, C. and Rosenberg, C. 1973, 'The female animal: Medical and biological views of woman and her role in nineteenth century America', *Journal of American History*, vol. 60, no. 2, pp. 332–56

Social Justice Collective (SJC), 1991, *Inequality in Australia*, Heinneman, Melbourne

Tepperman, L. 1994, *Choices and Chances: Sociology for everyday life*, 2nd edn, Harcourt Brace, Toronto

Theroux, P. 1992, *The Happy Isles of Oceania: Paddling the Pacific*, Penguin, London

Thompson, E. P. 1967, 'Time, work, discipline and industrial capitalism', *Past and Present*, no. 38, pp. 56–96

Turner, B. 1992, *Regulating Bodies: Essays in medical sociology*, Routledge, London

——1997, 'Understanding Change: Modernity and post-modernity' in Jureidini, R., Kenny, S. and Poole, M. (eds), *Sociology: Australian Connections*, Allen & Unwin, Sydney, pp. 117–38

——(ed), 2006, *The Cambridge Dictionary of Sociology*, Cambridge University Press, Cambridge

Turtle, A., Ford, B., Habgood, R., Grant, M., Bekiaris, J., Constantinou, C., Macek, M. and Polyzoidis, H., 1989, 'AIDS related beliefs and behaviours of Australian university students', *The Medical Journal of Australia*, vol. 150, 3 April, pp. 371–6

UNAIDS/World Health Organization (WHO), 2002, *Global Summary of the HIV/AIDS Epidemic*, Geneva <www.unaids.org/worldaidsday/2002/press/update/epiupdate2002_en.doc> [17 October 2003]

UNHIV/AIDS, 2009, *09 AIDS Epidemic Update Joint United Nations Programme on HIV/AIDS (UNAIDS) and WHO*, December <www.who.int/hiv/data/en> [1 May 2010]

United Nations International Children's Emergency Fund (UNICEF), 1994, *State of the World's Children*, New York

Urry, J. 1990, *The Tourist Gaze: Leisure and travel in contemporary societies*, Sage, London

Vera, H. 1989, 'On Dutch windows', *Qualitative Sociology*, vol. 12, no. 2, pp. 215–34

Vox T., Barker B., Stanley L., Lopez A. 2007 *Burden of disease and injury in Aboriginal and Torres Strait Islander peoples: 2003*. Brisbane: Centre for Burden of Disease and Cost-Effectiveness: School of Population Health, University of Queensland

Waldron, I. 1983, 'The role of genetic and biological factors in sex differences and mortality' in Lopez, A. D. and Ruzicka, L. T. (eds.) *Sex Differences in Mortality*, Department of Demography, Australian National University, Canberra

Waters, M. and Crook, R. 1990, *Sociology One*, Longman Cheshire, Melbourne

Whiting, R. 1979, 'You've gotta have 'wa'', *Sports Illustrated*, 24 September, pp. 60–71

Willis, E. 1994, 'The changing social relations of condom technology in the AIDS era' in Willis, E. (ed.) *Illness and Social Relations: Issues in the sociology of health care*, Allen & Unwin, Sydney, pp. 114–32

World Bank, 2000, 'World Development Indicators', Washington, DC

World Health Organization (WHO), 2002, 'AIDS Epidemic Update', December, WHO Office of HIV/AIDS and Sexually Transmitted Diseases, Geneva <www.who.int/hiv/en/> [17 September 2004]

World Wildlife Foundation (WWF), 2000, 'Population Estimates of Existing Wild Tigers in 2000', <www.worldwildlife.org/tigers/population.cfm> [2 February 2002]

Wright Mills, C. 1959, *The Sociological Imagination*, Penguin, New York

Index